ENDORSE

M000027494

"David Steele's *Bold Reformer* is a book for our times! As we celebrate the 500th anniversary of the Reformation, how appropriate to look afresh at ways the bold faith and action of Martin Luther can inspire and instruct our own faith and work. Christians today need strength of character and boldness of conviction. Steele's presentation of Luther's life moves readers to live bold lives that adorn the gospel of grace alone, by faith alone, in Christ alone."

Dr. Bruce A. Ware, T. Rupert and Lucille Coleman Professor of Christian Theology, Chairman of the Department of Christian Theology, The Southern Baptist Theological Seminary

"Pastoral ministry is often mingled with both blessing and despair. Many pastors experience seasons of opposition that result in discouragement and even depression. David Steele's new work *Bold Reformer* is an exploration into the gospel-centered convictions of the stalwart reformer, Martin Luther. Luther faced many pastoral hardships during his ministry, but emerged victorious because of his unwavering faith in the gospel of Jesus Christ. I encourage you to drink from the refreshing waters of this book and use the life of

Luther as an example that emboldens you to stand strong in the midst of the fiery trial."

Dr. Steven J. Lawson, President, OnePassion Ministries, Dallas, Texas

"This book could not have come at a better time. More than ever, today's pastors and church leaders need the boldness of Martin Luther set on display in this book. May God raise up another generation of bold reformers!"

Jeremy Pickens, Senior Pastor, Good Shepherd Community Church, Ferndale, Washington

"I read Dr. Steele's book *Bold Reformer* while in the middle of a preaching series on the book of Daniel entitled "Thriving in Babylon." I live in one of the least churched areas of North America. Reading this book spurred me on in my calling to be a Bold Reformer in the ilk of Martin Luther. Jesus wants his disciples to thrive—and *Bold Reformer* shows us how to thrive in the midst of exile in our own "Babylons"—biblically, theologically, Christo-centrically, gospel-focused, and practically for God's glory!"

Dr. David P. Craig, Lead Pastor, Valley Baptist Church, San Rafael, California

"In an age when God's Word is mocked and maligned from inside and outside the church, the pastor/teacher needs the courage to persevere in the faithful proclamation of God's Word. Dr. David Steele's book *Bold Reformer* will embolden the preacher/servant to be steadfast and immovable when challenged by the scandalous scoffs of post-modernity. Using Luther's brazen example for his template, this book is a must read for every pastor, elder, and proclaimer of truth! Thank you, David, for sharing your story and passion for the gospel, and for using church history to equip us for the work we must all do today!"

Bruce Parker, Pastor, Faith Bible Church, Hood River, Oregon

"Dr. Steele has done a wonderful job of documenting and drawing distinct parallels between what Martin Luther was encountering and our contemporary shallow biblical teaching. It is this shallowness that has born all sorts of aberrant teachings similar to the Roman Catholic Church in Martin Luther's day. Dr. Steele is correct in stating that it is time for true believers to step forward and become bold reformers and defend the true biblical faith. This is a book that evangelical leaders should be reading."

Ken Chin, Bionex Solutions Inc., San Jose, California

Bold Reformer: Celebrating the Gospel-Centered Convictions of Martin Luther

ISBN 10: 1-63296-070-2

ISBN 13: 978-1-63296-070-2

eISBN10: 1-63296-071-0

eISBN 13: 978-1-63296-071-9

Special Sales: Most Lucid Books titles are available in special quantity discounts. Custom imprinting or excerpting can also be done to fit special needs. Contact Lucid Books at info@lucid-books.net.

Unless otherwise noted, all English definitions are from New Oxford American Dictionary, 3rd ed., and all Greek definitions are cited from James A. Swanson, Dictionary of Biblical Languages with Semantic Domains: Greek (New Testament) (Oak Harbor: Logos Research Systems, Inc., 1997), Logos Library System.

BOLD
REFORMER

DAVID S. STEELE

To
Pastor Wayne Pickens -

*For modeling a life of godliness and humility
in the home and the church;
for molding me with tough love and tender love;
for mentoring me in pastoral ministry;
for mobilizing my head, heart, feet, and hands for the
shepherding challenge;
for marching with me during dark days;
for teaching me to be tough as nails, yet mourn over sin;
and for leading, feeding, and protecting the people of God
with the resolve of a bold reformer.*

Soli Deo gloria!

CONTENTS

FOREWORD

Our family had just moved to a small town and I had a new job as a senior administrator at a small regional state university when I met Dr. David Steele. At the time, he was serving as the Pastor of Theology at a church we visited, and eventually joined. That was the beginning of my appreciation of his love for the gospel of Jesus Christ, and his commitment to be a student and teacher of God's Word. My friendship with and appreciation for Dr. Steele has continued to grow over the past twelve years as I've witnessed him and his family grow in their faith, endure hardships, and remain faithful in chaos. He lives what he preaches and is a good example of a *bold reformer.*

This book, *Bold Reformer: Celebrating the Gospel-Centered Convictions of Martin Luther*, reminds us of the conviction, boldness, and courage of the sixteenth-century monk whose life was transformed by the truth of God's Word. The story is an inspiration for those of us who live in a culture with the dangerous assumption that, in the American dream, our greatest asset is our own ability. The American dream prizes what people can accomplish when they believe in themselves and trust in themselves, and we are drawn toward such thinking. But the gospel of Jesus Christ beckons us to die to ourselves and to believe in God and to trust in his power. In the gospel, God confronts us with our utter inability to accomplish anything of value apart from him.

David Platt captures this well in his book *Radical: Taking Back Your Faith from the American Dream*, 493 years after Luther took back the gospel of Jesus Christ with the truth of grace alone, through faith alone, in Christ alone from a church culture of good deeds, apostasy, and corruption.

We live in a post-Christian culture in 2016 America, and things are not trending in the direction of Bible-believing, Jesus-loving, sin-repenting, mission-serving Christianity. We have more biblical ignorance in our churches than at any other time in our country's history, and serious Christ-followers are a minority in an increasingly hostile host culture.

Dr. Steele directs us where Luther went almost five hundred years ago, the truth that our salvation comes not from our own abilities or efforts, but by God's amazing grace (Titus 3:5), and that "the righteous shall live by faith" (Romans 1:16-17). Biblical Christianity calls us to repent of both unrighteous sin and self-righteous religion. Readers of this book will be reminded of truths that are as relevant, timely, and compelling today as they were when first nailed to the Wittenberg church doors.

We need revival, a reformation of our hearts and minds. We don't need more self-help books, we don't need more welfare programs or feel-good efforts: we need more of Jesus Christ. Our battleground is not marriage, sexuality, sanctity of life, justice, or hunger. Our battleground is the gospel. Jesus is enough.

I applaud Dr. Steele for this book of stories and reminders of a historical shift in the understanding of, and appreciation for, God's Word, and I highly recommend this book. I have worked with university students for thirty-three years. My hope and prayer is that these amazingly bright, motivated, and capable young men and women will have hearts of courage to turn this county from materialistic, individualistic idolatry to a commitment to God's Word, to truth, fidelity, and a high opinion of God without compromise—to be bold reformers. To Christ be all glory.

Sheldon C. Nord, Ph.D.
President
Corban University
Salem, Oregon

INTRODUCTION

The winter of 2014 was one of the stormiest seasons of my life. The church God called me to pastor walked through a season of bitter adversity that resulted in a church split. Friendships were broken. Trust was shattered. The character of some godly men I love dearly was attacked. Lies were uttered. Mass emails were sent with damaging rhetoric and propaganda. People left the church and the pastor was discouraged.

I was the demoralized pastor. I was marginalized and I experienced betrayal. Simple tasks became overwhelming obstacles to overcome. The joy of ministry evolved into duty-driven drudgery.

I feared entering the pulpit. I had dreams of ecclesiastical assassination—either the "kill-shot" that explodes from the lips of carnal professors or the kind that is fired from the barrel of a gun. I recall being paralyzed with fear one particular morning, moments before the message I was scheduled to preach. During the song that preceded the sermon, I sat down to collect my thoughts. I prayed for mercy. I prayed for strength. I prayed for boldness and courage. The song concluded and the worship director led in prayer. The hand of a dear woman behind me rested on my shoulder as if to communicate support and to assure me that at least one person was praying. At least one person could understand my fear and anxiety.

My fear was not an isolated event. My family also endured many days of uncertainty and anguish. They were troubled by the accusations that were aimed in my direction. They were disheartened by the anger that erupted from the mob. They felt the sting of betrayal. They had questions. Their father and husband did not have many answers.

As I weighed the options before me, the future was not glowing with optimism. False accusations continued. The sanctuary attendance became more sparse. The "boa constrictor" of insecurity threatened to squeeze the life out of me. I recall one weekend when I endured several hours of throbbing head pain that I've never experienced in my life. That night I was plagued with dreams of parishioners who confronted me and accused me of being a horrible pastor. I was actually concerned for my own safety. I remember waking early on Sunday morning and believing the lies that tormented me in my dreams.

For me, those days were filled with hopelessness and replete with a sense of dread. The weight seemed unbearable and threatened to crush me with the force of a small army.

Most pastors can understand the overwhelming burden of shepherding a church. The events that occurred early in 2014 only added to the heavy load and several times I was tempted to throw in the towel. This pastor was at the end of his ecclesiastical rope—that is, until I began to consider the way of the bold reformer.

TWO DAYS, ONE IDEA

I experienced what some refer to as the "dark night of the soul." I was growing more and more discouraged as the false accusations continued. More people left the church. Some say that leadership is lonely. That is an understatement. Loneliness is only the tip of the iceberg.

In the midst of this adversity, there was a commitment to develop a long-range strategic plan for the church. The planning team was assembled several months before the storm struck and was even temporarily set aside for many weeks during the most difficult days of the ordeal. The temptation to focus on the distant future, however, and ignore the brewing tempest of the crisis at hand was almost irresistible.

The pressure was mounting and I was losing ground. In somewhat of a last-ditch effort, I arranged to spend two days at a retreat center where I would focus my prayer, energy, and attention on the strategic plan. Hours before I arrived at the retreat center, my back went out. Searing pain like I had never experienced pulsated in my lower back. I purchased some over-the-counter pain medication to help alleviate the throbbing. Nothing helped and the pain persisted.

I made my way to the retreat center and began the process of writing the strategic plan, which would guide the church for years to come. I was

convinced of the importance of the process. Yet, I
was hopelessly "stuck in the mud" and searching for
direction. I was a sole traveler on a country road,
boxed in by the "fog of adversity" which clouded
my mind, hindered my passion, and prevented any
real progress from taking place.

Thankfully, the plan began to take shape, by
God's grace and mercy. I started to type words
that would soon become the mission and vision of
Christ Fellowship.

*The **MISSION** of Christ Fellowship is to
help people become fully devoted followers of
Jesus Christ.*

*Our **VISION** is to be a **high-commit-
ment**, **high-grace** family of Christ-
followers who strive to live **gospel-driven**
and **God-centered** lives, **equipped** to
reach our community and the nations with the
saving message of the gospel.*

Crafting the mission and vision statements
was incredibly encouraging and affirming. There
was a new resolve in my attitude as the document
continued to develop. Later that evening, an email
came from one of the members of the planning
team. Words of affirmation jumped off the
computer screen as my friend expressed appreciation for a recent difficult decision I had made
and how it had brought "healing" to the church

family.[1] She wrote, "Thank you for your boldness to continue to lead us through the tough times. We are growing and learning. "The *Bold Reformer*" should be your email address!"[2]

There are pivotal moments in the history of any local church that are turning points or watersheds in their life story. At times, events occur that are pregnant with possibilities and implications for the future that will forever alter the direction of the church as it moves toward its God-intended destiny.

THE SHAPE OF THE BOLD REFORMER

Church history showcases an unbroken line of bold reformers—men who were willing to die for the sake of truth; men of courage and conviction; men who embraced Scripture: men like Athanasius, William Tyndale, Jan Hus, and John Rogers. These men said what they meant and meant what they said. They refused to capitulate or waver. Their biblical values outweighed cultural norms. Their biblical convictions towered above the speculations of worldly men. Their rock-solid adherence to Scripture never faded. These were men of certainty—men who were captured by a biblical worldview; men who were persuaded by divine reality. These godly men were Christ-centered and

---

1. Thanks to Beth Strotz for the email and for providing the inspiration for the book.
2. My email address has been baldreformer@gmail.com for years. One letter can make all the difference. Just ask Athanasius!

they loved the gospel of the Lord Jesus Christ. And their fidelity to truth was a banner that rose high above the musings of men and the philosophers of this age. Indeed, these men believed with the apostles, "We must obey God rather than men" (Acts 5:29).

Martin Luther was such a man. He was a bold reformer. Luther was born in Eisleben, Germany, on November 10, 1483. In 1501, he enrolled at the University of Erfurt. Four years later, he walked away with a B.A. (1502) and an M.A. (1505). He was prepared to take the next step in his academic career—the field of law.

His aspirations to study law were short-lived, however, as he was taken by surprise in a violent thunderstorm on July 2, 1505. Afraid for his life, he cried out in a last-ditch effort, "St. Anne, help me! I will become a monk!"

Unlike many people who make desperate promises to God, Luther kept his word. Two weeks later, he made plans to enter the monastery. His decision deeply disturbed his father, who had arranged his son's ascent into the field of law.

Luther's days in the monastery were rigorous to say the least: "His days as a novice were occupied with those religious exercises designed to [flood] the soul with peace. Prayers came seven times daily. After eight hours of sleep, the monks were awakened between one and two in the morning by the ringing of the cloister bell."[3] While these religious activities were designed to bring peace to the soul of the budding monk, they only brought more despair.

The next thunderstorm occurred at the occasion of his first mass. The date was May 2, 1507. Luther uttered these words: "We offer unto thee, the living, the true, the eternal God..." And the young monk froze! He admitted afterward,

> At these words I was utterly stupefied and terror-stricken. I thought to myself, 'With what tongue shall I address such Majesty, seeing that all men ought to tremble in the presence of even an earthly prince? Who am I, that I should lift up mine eyes or raise my hands to the divine Majesty? The angels surround him. At his nod the earth trembles. And shall I, a miserable little pygmy, say 'I want this, I ask for that?' For I am dust and ashes and full of sin and I am speaking to the living, eternal and the true God.'[4]

Having faced a second thunderstorm, Luther vowed to work even harder to earn God's favor. He fasted for days on end. He slept in the snow without the comfort of blankets. Some days he would be proud of his personal holiness and would say, "I have done nothing wrong today." But for all his so-called "works of righteousness," he still

---

3. Roland Bainton, *Here I Stand* (New York: Abingdon Press, 1950), 27.
4. Ibid., 30.

questioned the adequacy of his efforts. Had he fasted enough? Had he prayed enough? Had he worked hard enough to earn the favor of a holy God?

Years later, Luther contemplated those early years as a monk,

> I myself was a monk for twenty years. I tortured myself with praying, fasting, keeping vigils, and freezing—the cold alone was enough to kill me—and I inflicted upon myself such pain as I would never inflict again, even if I could...If any monk ever got to heaven by monkery, then I should have made it. All my monastery companions who knew me can testify to that.[5]

Luther's spiritual frustrations continued to gain momentum and intensify. His pilgrimage to Rome in 1510 did not help. He was shocked by the rampant ungodliness that ruled the city. He was horrified by some of the priests he met. But it was the selling of indulgences that truly made Luther's German blood boil! Pope Leo X had commissioned John Tetzel, the "telemarketer" of the day, to sell indulgences to the faithful. Indulgences were to be purchased for a given price and would reduce the time a loved one would spend in purgatory. Tetzel

5. Martin Luther, cited in Stephen J. Nichols, *Martin Luther: A Guided Tour of His Life and Thought* (Phillipsburg, PA: Presbyterian & Reformed, 2002), 29.

would cry out, "As soon as the coin in the coffer
rings, the soul from purgatory springs."

So, Luther was a man who was not only tempted
to despair, but he was also troubled by the ungodly
and unbiblical practices of a church he sought to
serve. And he was tormented by the notion of a
holy God who judges sin. He knew that if God
judged his sin, he would burn in hell forever.

Luther viewed God as a holy judge whom he
could never work hard enough to appease or please.
"Sometimes Christ seems to me nothing more than
an angry judge who comes to me with a sword in
His hand."[6] But everything changed in 1515.

Romans 1:16-17 changed the young monk's life:
*"For I am not ashamed of the gospel, for it is the power
of God for salvation to everyone who believes, to the Jew
first and also to the Greek. For in it the righteousness of
God is revealed from faith to faith, as it is written, 'The
righteous shall live by faith'"* (Rom. 1:16-17). Luther's
eyes instantly gravitated to verse 17—*"the righteous
shall live by faith."* He explains,

> My situation was that, although an im-
> peccable monk, I stood before God as
> a sinner troubled in conscience, and I
> had no confidence that my merit would
> assuage him. Therefore I did not love a
> just and angry God, but rather hated and
> murmured against him. Yet I clung to the

6. Martin Luther, cited in R. C. Sproul, *The Holiness of God* (Wheaton, IL:
Tyndale House, 1985), 75.

dear Paul and had a great yearning to
know what he meant.[7]

He continues,

> Night and day I pondered until I saw the
> connection between the justice of God
> and the statement that "the just shall live
> by his faith." Then I grasped the justice
> of God is that righteousness by which
> through grace and sheer mercy God
> justifies us through faith.

> Thereupon I felt myself to be reborn and
> to have gone through open doors into
> paradise. The whole Scripture took on a
> new meaning whereas before the "justice
> of God" had filled me with hate, now
> it became to me inexpressibly sweet in
> greater love. This passage of Paul became
> to me a gate to heaven.[8]

Luther understood that apart from justifying
grace, which pardoned his sin, he would never have
peace with God. Once he understood and embraced
the doctrine of justification by faith alone, he
was reconciled to a holy God. Once he accepted
the merits of Christ on his behalf, his sins were
forgiven; he had peace with God!

7. Martin Luther, cited in Roland Bainton, *Here I Stand*, 49-50.
8. Ibid.

A BOLD REFORMER IN WITTENBERG

Luther did not intend to break away from the Roman Catholic Church. He loved the church and had a deep desire to serve faithfully within the walls of his church. He earnestly sought to bring the church he loved into compliance with the Word of God. But God performed a miraculous work of grace in his heart that he could not deny. He began to spread the message of justification by faith alone. He taught it in the classroom. He proclaimed it from the pulpit.

Everything changed when he penned and posted his famous ninety-five theses to the castle door at Wittenberg on October 31, 1517. His action, in keeping with the tradition at the time, was to spark public debate. Thousands of copies were reprinted and distributed throughout Europe, thanks to the recent invention of the printing press. The Protestant Reformation was officially born as a mass of people learned that they could know God personally and be forgiven of all their sin—by grace alone, through faith alone, in Christ alone!

A BOLD REFORMER FOR THE WORLD

Luther's conversion ignited something powerful in his heart and mind. His ninety-five theses would spread far and wide. What began as a work of grace in the heart of a Roman Catholic monk soon spread like wildfire throughout Western Europe, and would eventually touch many parts of the world.

Luther continued to preach and teach boldly. He was compelled by God to speak the truth in dangerous times. In his short book *To the Christian Nobility of the German Nation*, Luther shared his passion and compulsion to teach the truth of God's Word:

> I know full well that I have been very out-spoken...I have attacked many things too severely. But how else ought I to do it? I am duty-bound to speak. If I had the power, these are the things I would do. I would rather have the wrath of the world upon me than the wrath of God. The world can do no more to me than take my life. In the past I have made frequent overtures of peace to my enemies, but as I see it, God has compelled me through them to keep on opening my mouth wider and wider and to give them enough to say, bark, shout, and write because they have nothing else to do.[9]

Martin Luther was a bold man. And a bold person, by definition, takes risks. A bold person is confident and courageous, willing to put his neck on the line. A bold person influences people and helps fan the flames of God's glory. In Luther's

---

9. Martin Luther, *To the Christian Nobility of the German Nation*, in *Three Treatises* (Minneapolis: Fortress Press, 1966), Kindle edition, Loc. 1183.

case, his bold influence was felt around the world and continues to shake the foundations of thinking people.

But Luther was committed to more than mere boldness. He was a bold *reformer*. By definition, a reformer is a catalyst to bring change. Reformers not only see God's desired future, they actually help create it. A reformer is not content with the status quo. A reformer has a heart for God and his people. A reformer sets the world on fire!

A fearless man of courage and conviction, Martin Luther was unstoppable. He was molded by the truth, convicted by truth, and changed by truth. Luther was tempered by the truth and transformed by the truth. He walked in the light and exposed the darkness, and he was unwilling to cower before men. He stood courageously before the most powerful men in the world, and he was unwilling to capitulate. He absolutely refused to compromise. This sixteenth-century man was a portrait of courage, a man driven by biblical conviction and compelled to spread it far and wide. Indeed, Martin Luther was a bold reformer for the world. With these thoughts in mind, we place our focus in this book as we celebrate the gospel-centered conviction of Martin Luther—the bold reformer.

CHAPTER ONE
RIPE FOR A NEW REFORMATION

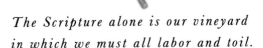

*The Scripture alone is our vineyard
in which we must all labor and toil.*

TO THE CHRISTIAN NOBILITY OF
THE GERMAN NATION,
AUGUST 1520

The Protestant Reformers were men of unbending principle. They were men of unyielding conviction. These men fought relentlessly for the truth. Some of the battle took place privately as godly men wrote books and treatises, which magnified the mighty work of the gospel. Much of the battle, however, took place in public as the reformers made their bold ascent into the pulpit. Lines were drawn, the Word of God was declared, and lives were forever changed.

A WILD BOAR IN THE VINEYARD

Martin Luther set the standard as the dawn of the Reformation began. He helped create the climate that made the Reformation possible.

On studying Luther's life and work, one thing is clear: the much-needed Reformation took place, not because Luther decided that it would be so, but rather because the time was ripe for it, and because the Reformer and many others were ready to fulfill their historical responsibility.[10]

But Luther's courageous act at Wittenberg was just the beginning. The newly reformed and converted monk continued to write and preach about the doctrines of grace. He continued to proclaim the doctrine of justification by faith alone, "the article upon which the church stands or falls," as Luther argued. He continued to warn people about the abuses of the Roman Catholic system, which was mired in works and corrupt to the core.

Luther's writing accelerated between 1517 and 1521 and would set the stage for the showdown at Worms, Germany. Three works in particular helped fuel the reformer's bold resolve as he made his stand before Rome. In August 1520, he published

---

10. Justo González, *The Story of Christianity, Volume 2: The Reformation to the Present Day* (San Francisco: HarperCollins Publishers, 1985), 15.

An Open Letter to the Christian Nobility, which refuted the medieval distinction between clergy and laity. He rejected the papal claim that suggested the pope is the only one who can interpret Scripture. In *An Open Letter to the Christian Nobility,* he exposed the corruption that saturated the Roman Catholic Church:

> Everything is controlled by those arch-villains at Rome, almost right down to the office of sexton and bell-ringer. Every dispute is called to Rome and everyone does just as he pleases, under cover of the pope's authority.[11]

> The arbitrary and deceptive reservation of the pope only creates a state of affairs in Rome that defies description. There is buying, selling, bartering, changing, trading, drunkenness, lying, deceiving, robbing, stealing, luxury, harlotry, knavery, and every sort of contempt of God. Even the rule of the Antichrist could not be more scandalous.[12]

Luther included several suggestions for ecclesiastical reform. One aspect of this reform included a commitment to Christian discernment. He writes, "We ought not to allow the Spirit of freedom to be frightened off by the fabrications of the popes, but we ought to march boldly forward and test all that

---

11. Martin Luther, *To the Christian Nobility of the German Nation,* in *Three Treatises,* Loc. 370.
12. Ibid., Loc. 424.

they do, or leave undone, by our believing understanding of the Scriptures."[13] This new spirit of discernment would begin in Germany and spread far and wide as the Reformation progressed.

That same year in October, Luther wrote *The Babylonian Captivity of the Church*, a scathing indictment of papal abuses. He says, "There is no doubt, therefore, that in our day all priests and monks, together with their bishops and all their superiors, are idolaters, living in a most perilous state by reason of this ignorance, abuse, and mockery of the mass, or sacrament, or promise of God."[14]

When Luther repudiated the Roman Catholic mass, he admitted the difficult nature of the task, especially since it has become so "thoroughly entrenched" in the church. But he understood the importance of standing for truth and being a bold reformer: "But my Christ lives, and we must be careful to give more heed to the Word of God than to all the thoughts of men and of angels."[15]

The Babylonian Captivity of the Church successfully exposed Rome and laid bare her sinful idolatry. Luther does not mince words in his exposé:

> For God does not deal, nor has he ever dealt, with man otherwise than through a word of promise, as I have said. We

---

13. Ibid., Loc. 220.
14. Martin Luther, *The Babylonian Captivity of the Church*, in *Three Treatises*, Kindle edition, Loc. 1663.
15. Ibid., Loc. 1571.

in turn cannot deal with God otherwise
than through faith in the Word of his
promise. He does not desire works, nor
has he need of them; rather we deal with
men and with ourselves on the basis of
works. But God has need of this: that
we consider him faithful in his promises
(Heb. 10:23), and patiently persists in
this belief, and thus worship him with
faith, hope, and love. It is in this way
that he obtains his glory among us, since
it is not ourselves who run, but of him
who shows mercy (Rom. 9:16), promises,
and gives, that we have and hold all good
things.[16]

Essentially, Luther argued that just as the
Jewish nation was swept into the grip of Babylon,
so too the Roman system had been taken captive
by the seduction of Babylon. The church had been
taken hostage by the Babylonian system—a system
of man-made rules, works, and traditions, a system
that fails to honor and glorify God.

Only weeks later, in November, Luther penned
The Freedom of a Christian. He continued to challenge
Pope Leo X, even though he included an open
letter, which was filled with conciliatory language.
In one of the challenges, Luther writes, "I have
been thoroughly incensed over the fact that good
Christians are mocked in your name and under the
cloak of the Roman church. I have resisted and will
continue to resist your see as long as the spirit of

---

16. Ibid., Loc. 1656-1663.

faith lives in me."[17] In another statement, Luther writes, "I have no quarrel with any man concerning his morals but only concerning the word of truth. In all other matters I will yield to any man whatsoever; but I have neither the power nor the will to deny the Word of God."[18]

These challenges were not only direct—they were relentless. The force of his arguments was bold and biblical. Luther wielded the mighty sword of God's Word like a battering ram, which infuriated Pope Leo and served to strengthen the resolve of God's people.

Luther's writings and passion for ecclesiastical reform enraged the pope. A papal bull was presented on June 15, 1520. The opening remarks reveal the escalating animosity between the pontiff and the bold reformer:

> Arise, O Lord, and judge thy cause. A wild boar has invaded thy vineyard. Arise, O Peter, and consider the case of the Holy Roman Church, the mother of all churches, consecrated by thy blood...Arise all ye saints, and the whole universal Church, whose interpretation of Scripture has been assailed...We can no longer suffer the serpent to creep through the field of the Lord. The books of Martin Luther which contain these errors are to be examined and burned...

---

17. Martin Luther, *The Freedom of a Christian*, in *Three Treatises* (Minneapolis: Fortress Press, 1966), Kindle edition, Loc. 2849.
18. Ibid., Loc. 2842.

Now therefore we give Martin sixty days in which to submit, dating from the time of the publication of this bull in his district. Anyone who presumes to infringe our excommunication and anathema will stand under the wrath of Almighty God and of the apostles Peter and Paul.[19]

So the stage was set. Luther was condemned as a heretic and excommunicated from the Roman Catholic Church. His books were burned in Rome. These were serious and sober days for the bold reformer. The response of Luther unveils his courage in these troubling times: "For me the die is cast. I despise alike Roman fury and Roman favor. I will not be reconciled or communicate with them. Let them damn and burn my books. I for my part, unless I cannot find a fire, will publicly damn and burn the whole canon law."[20]

It took nearly three months for the document to make it into Luther's hands. On October 10, 1520, Luther received the papal bull from the pope—*Exsurge Domine*. A sixty-day period of grace was extended to Luther, which would give him the chance to respond in a formal manner.

Luther's initial response is found in a letter he sent to Spalatin. In it, he refers to the pope as the "Antichrist." In one statement, Luther actually admits his error, but not in the way that the pope expected:

---

19. Luther, cited in Roland Bainton, *Here I Stand*, 114.
20. Ibid., 116.

I was wrong. I retract the statement that certain articles of John Hus are evangelical. I say now, 'Not some but all the articles of John Hus were condemned by Antichrist and his apostles in the synagogue of Satan.' And to your face, most holy Vicar of God, I say freely that all the condemned articles of John Hus are evangelical and Christian, and yours are downright impious and diabolical.[21]

Luther's formal response was even more vexing for the pope. For he not only responded with fiery words—he actually tossed the papal bull into the flames! Roland Bainton exposes Luther's public response:

Since they have burned my books, I burn theirs. The canon law was included because it makes the pope a god on earth. So far I have merely fooled with this business of the pope. All my articles condemned by Antichrist are Christian. Seldom has the pope overcome anyone with Scripture and with reason.[22]

So, with books ablaze on both sides of the ecclesiastical fence, the drama continued to unfold, a drama that would lead to a showdown in Worms. The bold reformer would face his most difficult challenge yet.

---

21. Ibid., 128.
22. Ibid.

THE WILD BOAR ARRIVES IN WORMS

The combination of Luther's ninety-five theses and his subsequent writing led to a theological tipping point. The pope summoned him to Worms where he would stand before the Roman authorities. Whether Luther would consent to the invitation was open to debate. But in a letter to Staupitz, the resolve of the bold reformer is clearly unveiled:

> This is not the time to cringe, but to cry aloud when our Lord Jesus Christ is damned, reviled, and blasphemed. If you exhort me to humility, I exhort you to pride. The matter is very serious. We see Christ suffer. If hitherto we ought to have been silent and humble, I ask you whether now, when the blessed Savior is mocked, we should not fight for him...I burned the pope's books at first with fear and trembling, but now I am lighter in heart than I have ever been in my life. They are so much more pestilent than I supposed.[23]

Clearly, Luther battles fear and anxiety as we shall see, but he remains undeterred as he consents to make the journey to Worms. In fact, his resolve appears to intensify as he nears his destination: "Unless I am held back by force, or Caesar revokes his invitation, I will enter Worms under the banner

---

23. Luther, cited in Roland Bainton, *Here I Stand*, 135.

of Christ against the gates of hell."[24] The courageous reformer made his way to the city of Worms,
Germany.

On April 16, 1521, the bold reformer arrived
at his appointed destination. Martin Luther would
stand before the church. He would make his
defense and justify his books, which stood diametrically opposed to the pope and the Roman system
of works.

Standing before the Archbishop, Luther was
faced with a stack of books and was challenged
directly with a pointed question: "Are these your
books?" And "do you recant?" At this moment,
Luther was anything but a bold reformer. Much
like his experience at his first Mass, he froze. The
accusers intimidated him. He understood the se-
riousness of the charges. He recognized that if
he denied the charges, he would not only stand in
disrepute among his supporters, but he would also
dishonor God. But any admission of guilt was tantamount to theological treason. His life was on the
line. Luther asked for a day to consider his reply.

One can only imagine what raced through
Luther's mind as he weighed the decision before
him. Clearly, fear and anxiety invaded his soul.
He was in a nearly impossible situation. But deep
in his heart, he knew how he would respond. He
would respond with courage. He would stand with
conviction. He would stand before the world as a
bold reformer.

---

24. Ibid., 139.

Once again, Luther faced his accusers: "Will you recant?" they questioned. Luther's response will be forever etched in church history and stands as a testament to his boldness and bravery:

> Since then your serene majesty and your lordships seek a simple answer, I will give it in this manner, plain and unvarnished: Unless I am convinced by the testimony of the Scriptures or by clear reason, for I do not trust either in the pope or in councils alone, since it is well known that they often err and contradict themselves, I am bound to the Scriptures I have quoted and my conscience is captive to the Word of God. I cannot and I will not retract anything, since it is neither safe nor right to go against conscience. I cannot do otherwise. Here I stand. May God help me, Amen.[25]

THE BOLD REFORMER ARRIVES IN WARTBURG

The story is well-known about how Luther's friend Fredrick the Wise arranged to have him "kidnapped" and whisked away in his journey from Worms to the Wartburg castle where he would spend the next ten months in seclusion. Luther spent these days mostly in isolation under the pseudonym, Junker Jörg.

He made good use of his time at Wartburg,

25. Luther, cited in Stephen J. Nichols, *The Reformation: How a Monk and a Mallet Changed the World* (Wheaton, IL: Crossway Books, 2007), 32.

translating the Greek New Testament into German, the language of the people. Luther spent hour after hour, laboring over the text and translating God's Word for the common man. Soon, thousands of people would read the Word of God in their mother tongue for the first time. They would hear the Word of God thunder from the pulpit in their heart language.

After his brief stop in Wartburg, Luther made his way back to Wittenberg where his reformation efforts continued. He "sought to persuade people," writes Michael Reeves, "with the Scriptures through simple, clear preaching. He believed that the word of God must first convince people, and then the rotten old structures would collapse."[26] Indeed, the Reformation tides continued to swell as the Word of God grew and people were transformed by God's Spirit.

THE NEED FOR BOLD REFORMERS IN THE 21st CENTURY

Nearly five hundred years have passed since Luther hammered his ninety-five theses on the castle door at Wittenberg. These days, some evangelicals are losing their theological nerve. Doctrinal propositions are being downplayed and even discarded. The historic creeds of the church

---

26. Michael Reeves, *The Unquenchable Flame: Discovering the Heart of the Reformation* (Nashville: B & H Academic, 2009), 56.

are being neglected, if not forgotten entirely. "No creed but Christ" is the new mantra. Drama and interpretive dance are in. Creeds and catechizing are relegated to the Stone Age.

I believe the time is ripe for a new Reformation. While some thinkers maintain the pointlessness of a new reformation, other theologians note the indispensability of one: "And in this age of religious pluralism, theological laxity, and biblical illiteracy, perhaps the Reformation is needed more than ever."[27] Perhaps a new reformation is on the horizon.

There is an urgent need for a new generation of bold reformers who dominate the theological landscape, which is drowning in compromise and capitulation. These leaders must be men and women of moral integrity and theological conviction. These people must be above reproach and accountable, and they must refuse to compromise the truth. They must refute the opposition, and they must rely on the power of the Holy Spirit. They must rest in the sovereignty of God. They must rejoice in the gospel, resolve to proclaim the gospel, and remember to stand firm in the gospel.

This book will address these critical issues, issues that face every Christ-follower who chooses to make an impact and make a difference in the twenty-first century. These are days when the

---

27. Stephen J. Nichols, *The Reformation: How a Monk and Mallet Changed the World* (Wheaton, IL: Crossway Books, 2007), 21.

people of God must stand and be counted. These are days that require courage and conviction. Our culture is starving for truth and thirsty for the Word of God. It is time for a new generation of bold reformers!

CHAPTER TWO
BOLD REFORMERS
RECOGNIZE THE NEED FOR REFORM

As soon as the coin in the coffer rings,
the soul from purgatory springs.

JOHN TETZEL

Martin Luther was a rebel. He was an outlaw who was an unworthy sinner. He was a tortured soul and he was a man who was tempted and tried. This was a man on the brink of despair. Although we have covered some of this history earlier, it bears repeating here.

The psychology of Luther is a conundrum, given his pedigree and educational background. At the age of twenty-one, he had already earned his Master's degree in law. Six months after graduating, he was caught in a thunderstorm, a storm that he assumed was the judgment of God that was about to crash on his head. He cried out, "Help me, St. Anne, and I will become a monk."

Luther kept his word and entered a strict Augustinian monastery and began his life as a monk in 1505. Roland Bainton observes, "His days as a novice were occupied with those religious exercises designed to [flood] the soul with peace. Prayers came seven times daily. After eight hours of sleep, the monks were awakened between one and two in the morning by the ringing of the cloister bell."[28] And while these religious activities were designed to bring peace to the soul of the budding monk, they only brought more disenchantment.

The next thunderstorm took place on the occasion of his first mass—May 2, 1507. Luther uttered these words: "We offer unto thee, the living, the true, the eternal God." And the young monk froze solid in his tracks. He admitted afterward:

> At these words I was utterly stupefied and terror-stricken. I thought to myself, 'With what tongue shall I address such Majesty, seeing that all men ought to tremble in the presence of even an earthly prince? Who am I, that I should lift up mine eyes or raise my hands to the divine Majesty? The angels surround him. At his nod the earth trembles. And shall I, a miserable little pygmy, say, 'I want this, I ask for that?' For I am dust and ashes and full

---

28. Bainton, *Here I Stand,* 27.

of sin and I am speaking to the living, eternal and the true God.'[29]

Having faced a second thunderstorm, Luther vowed to work hard to earn God's favor. He fasted days on end. He slept on snow without the comfort of blankets. Some days he would be so proud of his personal holiness and would opine, "I have done nothing wrong today." But despite his self-assurance, he found himself questioning his efforts. Had he fasted enough? Had he prayed enough? Had he worked hard enough to merit favor in the eyes of a holy God? Luther famously lamented, "I was a good monk, and I kept the rule of my order so strictly that I may say that if ever a monk got to heaven by his monkery it was I. All my brothers in the monastery who knew me will bear me out. If I had kept on any longer, I should have killed myself with vigils, prayers, reading, and other work."[30]

Luther's frustration only escalated when he took a pilgrimage to Rome in 1510. When he arrived, the piers for the new basilica of St. Peters had been recently constructed while the Sistine Chapel was not yet complete. He was shocked by the ungodliness of the city and the impiety of the priests he encountered. At one point, as Luther was performing the Mass, a priest whispered to him in Latin, "Get a move on."

29. Martin Luther, cited in ibid., 34.
30. Ibid., 34.

Additionally, the German monk was deeply disturbed by the practice of selling indulgences. Pope Leo X had commissioned John Tetzel to sell indulgences to the faithful. Indulgences were to be purchased for a price and would reduce the time a loved one would spend in purgatory. Tetzel would cry out, *"When a coin in the coffer rings, a soul from Purgatory springs."*[31]

So Luther was a man who was not only *tempted* to despair, but he was also *troubled* by the ungodly and unbiblical practices of a church he sought to faithfully serve. And he was *tormented* by the notion of a holy God who judges sin. He knew that if God judged his sin, he would be eternally condemned to hell! This is what haunted Luther the most. He saw God as a holy Judge whom he could never work hard enough to appease or please. He said, "Sometimes Christ seems to me nothing more than an angry judge who comes to me with a sword in His hand."[32]

LUTHER'S CONVERSION

Romans 1:16-17 is the passage that God sovereignly used to open the darkened eyes of this Roman Catholic monk: *"For I am not ashamed of the gospel, for it is the power of God for salvation to everyone*

---

31. Cited in Nichols, *The Reformation: How a Monk and a Mallet Changed the World*, 29.
32. Martin Luther, cited in Sproul, *The Holiness of God*, 75.

who believes, to the Jew first and also to the Greek. For in it the righteousness of God is revealed from faith for faith, as it is written, "The righteous shall live by faith." After explaining the relationship between the justice of God and the reality of Romans 1:16-17, Luther declared, "Thereupon I felt myself to be reborn and to have gone through open doors into paradise. The whole Scripture took on a new meaning, whereas before the justice of God had filled me with hate, now it became to me inexpressibly sweet in greater love. This passage of Paul became to me the gate to heaven."[33]

Luther understood that apart from justifying grace, which pardoned his sin, he would never have peace with God. Once he understood and embraced the doctrine of justification by faith alone—once he accepted the merits of Christ on his behalf—he was saved and had peace with God. Once Luther had right standing with God, he spread the message of justification by faith alone. It began in Wittenberg as he nailed his ninety-five theses to the door of the castle church, prompting vigorous debate. Thousands of copies were reprinted and distributed throughout Europe. Luther's books and sermons were published far and wide. And the Protestant Reformation was officially born as people everywhere learned that they could know God personally and be forgiven of all their sins by grace alone, through faith alone, in Christ alone!

---

33. Martin Luther, cited in Bainton, *Here I Stand*, 49-50.

Crucial Pillars of Justification

Notice four pillars of justification that grew out of Luther's conversion experience. These pillars form the unshakable foundation that every follower of Christ clings to and cherishes.

Pillar 1: The Motive for Justification

There is a three-fold motive for justification that shapes our understanding of this all-important doctrine. First, every person is a sinner by nature and choice. *"Therefore, just as sin came into the world through one man, and death through sin, and so death spread to all men because all sinned"* (Rom. 5:12).

Second, every person is dead in sin and enslaved to sin. Ephesians 2:1 reminds us, *"And you were dead in the trespasses and sins in which you once walked, following the course of this world, following the prince of the power of the air, the spirit that is now at work in the sons of disobedience."* John 8:34 adds, *"Truly, truly, I say to you, everyone who practices sin is a slave to sin."* Jesus makes it clear that every sinner is in bondage to sin, helpless and hopeless apart from grace.

Third, every sinner is destined for judgment apart from the grace of God. Romans 2:8 warns, *"But for those who are self-seeking and do not obey the truth, but obey unrighteousness, there will be wrath and fury."*

Pillar 2: The Meaning of Justification

The biblical notion of righteousness comes from the Greek term *dikaiosune*, which involves purity of life and integrity. "It is the condition of rightness; that standard of which is God, which is estimated according to the divine standard."[34] Wayne Grudem explains, "God's righteousness means that God always acts in accordance with what is right and is himself the final standard of what is right."[35]

When God justifies the sinner, he imparts the very righteousness of God to the undeserving sinner. In justification, God forgives our sin and declares us righteous. R.C. Sproul refers to justification as the "act by which unjust sinners are made right in the sight of a just and holy God."[36] So sinners receive God's righteousness, a gift that can never be earned.

When the sinner is justified, he is rescued from the consequences of sin (Rom. 6:23). He is set free from the guilt of sin (Eph. 1:7; Col. 1:14), the power of sin (Rom. 6:6), the penalty of sin (Eph. 2:5-6), the pollution of sin (Rom. 6:6), and he will one day be delivered from the very presence of sin. Additionally, he is redeemed from the slavery of sin (John 8:34; Gal. 5:1), and the wrath of God (Eph. 2:3).

The sinner, as noted above, is granted the very righteousness of God by faith alone (Rom. 3:21-26;

34. Kenneth Wuest, *Romans in the Greek New Testament* (Grand Rapids: Eerdmans, 1955), 27.

35. Wayne Grudem, *Systematic Theology* (Grand Rapids: Zondervan Publishing House, 1994), 203.

36. R. C. Sproul, *Essential Truths of the Christian Faith* (Wheaton, IL: Tyndale, 1998), 189.

5:1). Every justified person is now free to fellowship with God (Eph. 2:13) and receives eternal life (Col. 3:1-4). This doctrine was so important to Luther that he announced, "The doctrine of justification by faith alone is the article upon which the church stands or falls."[37]

Pillar 3: The Means of Justification

The necessary condition for justification is *faith alone*. Once again, the apostle declares, "*For in it the righteousness of God is revealed from faith for faith, as it is written, "The righteous shall live by faith"*" (Rom. 1:17). He continues in Romans 5:1, "*Therefore, since we have been justified by faith, we have peace with God through our Lord Jesus Christ.*"

Yet despite the clear teaching of Scripture, Rome insisted that works are necessary to receive justifying grace:

> If anyone saith, that by faith alone the impious is justified; in such wise as to mean that nothing else is required to co-operate in order to the obtaining the grace of Justification, and that it is not in any way necessary, that he be prepared and disposed by the movement of his own will; let him be anathema (*Council of Trent, Canons on Justification, Canon 14*).
>
> If anyone saith, that man is truly absolved from his sins and justified, because he

37. Luther, cited in Alistair McGrath, *Christian Theology* (Oxford: Blackwell Publishing, 2001), 480.

assuredly believed himself absolved and justified; or, that no one is truly justified but he believes himself justified; and that, by this faith alone absolution and justification are effected; let him be anathema (*Council of Trent, Canons on Justification, Canon 14*).

Notice that Rome not only denied that justification is by faith alone, but she also anathematized anyone who claimed to be justified by faith alone!

Luther learned that faith alone has *always* been the necessary condition for one's sins to be forgiven. Reaching as far back as Genesis, he discovered that even Abraham was justified by faith alone. "*And he believed the LORD, and he counted it to him as righteousness*" (Gen. 15:6).

And make no mistake: Luther did not discover this precious doctrine. He rediscovered it! He unearthed the doctrine that had been buried for hundreds of years of church history. When he rediscovered the doctrine of justification, he was able to answer the question that reverberated throughout Europe, namely—*How can a sinful person stand in the presence of a holy God?* The answer: sinners are justified by grace alone through faith alone in Christ alone!

Pillar 4: The Magnitude of Justification

We have seen the motive for justification. We have reviewed the meaning of justification and the means of justification. Now we must consider the magnitude of justification.

The magnitude of justification cannot be over-stated. This doctrine is an earth-shattering reality, a reality which must be embraced, treasured, and proclaimed. The Scriptures proclaim that justification is for everyone who believes, *"to the Jew first and also to the Greek"* (Rom. 1:16b; c.f. Acts 13:47). For every person who confesses his or her sin before a holy God, this gospel is for you! For every person who acknowledges they have transgressed the holy law of God and spurned the greatness of his worth, this gospel is for you!

If you are trusting in your "good works" in an effort to please God, the Bible commands you to *repent*. If you are banking on a religious family to gain entrance into the kingdom of God, the Bible commands you to *repent*. If you are like Luther prior to his conversion, the Bible urges you to turn from your sins and trust Christ alone for salvation!

So Luther finally understood that works could never save him, religion could never place him in right standing before God. He learned his so-called "righteousness" was not only unacceptable to God—it was repugnant to God. The monk turned Reformer rediscovered the doctrine of justification by faith alone. That message would spread like wildfire throughout Europe and the rest of the world, breaking the back of the Roman system of works.

LUTHER'S CHALLENGE:
THE NEED FOR A REFORMED CHURCH

In the sixteenth century, Luther identified the areas where the church needed to be reformed. The word *reformation* comes from the Latin verb, *reformo*, which means "to form again, mold anew, or revive." In our day, there is an ongoing need for the church to be remolded and revived. There is an urgent need for reformation in the church of Jesus Christ. So, with Luther and the Protestant Reformers, bold reformers *recognize the need for reform*. Just as Luther spoke truth to power in his day, the contemporary church needs courageous spokespeople to identify specific abuses and offer positive solutions now to transform the church of today. Three specific areas need reformation.

Our View of God Must Be Reformed

First, our view of God must be reformed. We live in a culture where the doctrine of God is constantly under fire. Open theists attack God's comprehensive foreknowledge. Modalists deny the distinctions in the Trinity and denounce the Trinity. Inclusivists reject the exclusivity of Jesus Christ. And many evangelicals embrace a vision of God that is captivated by his love but casts aside any notion of wrath or eternal judgment.

A.W. Tozer understands the importance of a high view of God, a view of God, which must be constantly reforming:

> What comes into our minds when we think about God is the most important thing about us...So necessary to the Church is a lofty concept of God that when that concept in any measure declines, the Church with her worship and her moral standards declines along with it. The first step down for any church is taken when it surrenders its high opinion of God.[38]

Four strategic initiatives will help ensure our view of God is always reforming:

1. Recover Our Vision of God's Greatness

Evangelicals in droves have tragically failed to heed A.W. Tozer's warning. We have, in large measure, failed to teach a robust doctrine of God. We have not communicated successfully about a God who is sovereign over all things (Ps. 115:3; Ps. 24:8); a God who reigns over the nations and over the affairs of men (Ps. 99:1; Prov. 21:1). We have neglected the lordship of God (Ps. 24:1-2). We have failed to learn about and magnify a God who is beautiful beyond measure (Ps. 27:4). We have failed to worship this God who is glorious and majestic (Exod. 15:11). We have lost our vision of God's greatness.

Over and over again, the Scriptures draw our attention to the greatness of God. Psalm 99:2 says, *"The LORD is great in Zion; he is exalted over all the*

---

38. A.W. Tozer, *The Knowledge of the Holy* (Lincoln, NE: Back to the Bible, 1961), 1, 4.

peoples" (Ps. 99:2). Psalm 135:5 continues, "*For I know that the LORD is great, and that our Lord is above all gods.*" Reforming our view of God, therefore, involves recovering our vision of the greatness of God.

2. Recover Our Thirst for God's holiness.

We must reclaim and recover our thirst for the holiness of God. Moses was instructed by God, "*Do not come near, take your sandals off your feet, for the place on which you are standing is holy ground*" (Exod. 3:5). Uzzah paid the ultimate price for disregarding the holiness of God (2 Sam. 6:6-7). Isaiah modeled a thirst for holiness as he encountered God: "*And I said: "Woe is me! For I am lost; for I am a man of unclean lips, and I dwell in the midst of a people of unclean lips; for my eyes have seen the King, the LORD of hosts!*" (Isa. 6:5).

Many evangelicals have more in common with Uzzah as they downplay or even disregard God's transcendent holiness. Our approach to God is casual; our prayers border on irreverent. Contemporary worship often neglects the transcendence of God, which by default minimizes the greatness of his worth. "Me" has replaced "Thee," as the holiness of God moves to the perimeter of the sanctuary and makes preparation to depart, indefinitely. Indeed, the glory has departed. When all eyes are on the creature and the Creator is neglected, our thirst for holiness must be recovered. "*Exalt the LORD our God*" cries the psalmist.

"Worship at his footstool! Holy is he" (Ps. 99:5). As we recover our thirst for the holiness of God, so too will we begin to reform our view of God!

3. Recover Our Passion for God's Glory

We must also recover our passion for the glory of God. The term *glory* means "weightiness or heaviness." It makes reference to the honor of God and his presence, which is manifested in power. Isaiah says, *"For my own sake, for my own sake, I do it, for how should my name be profaned? My glory I will not give to another"* (Isa. 48:11).

Carl Trueman agrees with Luther that every sermon must "destroy self-righteousness and point hearers toward the alien, external righteousness of Christ...He must hold before the congregation a vision of the transcendent glory and holiness of God, and force congregants to see just how catastrophically far short of that they all fall."[39] Tragically, in an attempt to garner the praise and approval of men, many sermons miss the mark and fail to glorify the living God.

The triune God must be the chief object of our affections. He must become the focus of our thoughts. Indeed, the great and glorious God of the universe must be our consuming passion. The psalmist writes, *"As the deer pants for flowing streams, so pants my soul for you, O God. My soul thirsts for God,*

---

39. Carl R. Trueman, *Luther on the Christian Life* (Wheaton, IL: Crossway Books, 2015), 92.

for the living God. When shall I come and appear before God? (Ps. 42:1-2). *"Whom have I in heaven but you? And there is nothing on earth that I desire besides you"* (Ps. 73:25). We must recover our passion for God's glory in order to sufficiently reform our view of God.

4. *Recover Our Holy Fear of God*

John Calvin writes, "[We should] restrain ourselves from sinning not out of dread of punishment alone; but because [we] love and revere God as Father, [and] worship and adore him as Lord. Even if there were no hell, it would still shudder at offending him alone."[40] Calvin reminds us that we must recover our holy fear of God.

We have a propensity to distort the biblical vision of God. We downplay his authority. We short-circuit his sovereignty, his supreme power and authority. In an attempt to emphasize his immanence, or the pervasive closeness of his presence, we often neglect his transcendence, the fact that he is incomparable and without equal. And we search for ways to make his standards more palatable. However, R.C. Sproul reminds us, "God does not lower his standards to accommodate us."[41] He will not tolerate a compromise of his character.

One way we can recover our holy fear of God is

---

40. John Calvin, *Institutes of the Christian Religion* (Philadelphia: Westminster Press, 1536), 43.
41. Sproul, *The Holiness of God*, 88.

by preaching and teaching about the wrath of God. Once again, Trueman casts light on this important subject. He highlights the reluctance of our culture to acknowledge that God is holy and deserves to be feared. He adds, "Luther's doctrine of justification depends upon two things: the constant preaching of the wrath of God in the face of sin; and the re-alization that every Christian is at once righteous and a sinner, thus needing the hammer of the law to terrify and break the sinful conscience."[42] Sadly, some Christians shy away from this God-centered counsel and minimize God's wrath at best or even discard it all together. The net result is a devastat-ing blow to the cause of Christ. To remove God's wrath is tantamount to theological treason.

Our view of God must be reformed by recover-ing our vision of God's greatness, recovering our thirst for God's holiness, recovering our passion for God's glory, and recovering our holy fear of God. A key aspect of this commitment is to warn sinners that God is angry with sin and will unleash his wrath on the unrepentant. But we must move to another crucial step in the reformation process—namely, the reformation of our view of sin.

Our View of Sin Must Be Reformed

Second, our view of sin must be reformed. Luther remarks, "Though I lived as a monk without reproach, I felt I was a sinner before God with

---

42. Trueman, *Luther on the Christian Life*, 174.

an extremely disturbed conscience."[43] The German reformer believed that the very act of confessing our sinfulness is in itself an act of faith: "By faith alone it must be believed that we are sinners, and indeed more often than not we seem to know nothing against ourselves. Wherefore we must stand by God's judgment and believe his words by which he calls us unrighteous."[44]

Notice several resolutions, which will serve bold reformers well as we move toward a reformed view of sin.

1. Resolve to Embrace a Biblical Understanding of Sin

"Sin is transgression of the revealed will of God which teaches that we are to act in perfect holiness from a heart of faith to the glory of God."[45] Scripture clearly teaches us that sinners are born, not made. In other words, each person is born with radical depravity. David makes this well-known lament: *"Behold, I was brought forth in iniquity, and in sin did my mother conceive me"* (Ps. 51:5). Each one of us, therefore, is a sinner both by nature and by choice. Jeremiah affirms, *"The heart is deceitful above all things, and desperately sick; who can understand it?"* (Jer. 17:9). Isaiah underscores this truth as well: *"We have all become like one who is unclean, and all our righteous deeds are like a polluted garment. We all*

---

43. Martin Luther, cited in Nichols, *The Reformation*, 30.
44. Martin Luther, cited in Bainton, *Here I Stand*, 176.
45. John Piper, *A Baptist Catechism* (Minneapolis: Desiring God Ministries), 8.

*fade like a leaf, and our iniquities, like the wind, take us
away"* (Isa. 64:6).

Apart from grace, each of us is dead in trespasses and enslaved to the tyranny of sin. We are
destined for judgment in hell apart from Christ
and the benefits of his saving work on the cross.
Jonathan Edwards reminds us of our true condition
apart from grace: "There are the black clouds of
God's wrath now hanging directly over your heads,
full of the dreadful storm, and big with thunder;
and were it not for the restraining hand of God, it
would immediately burst forth upon you."[46]

Embracing a biblical understanding of sin is
a vivid reminder of where we stand apart from
grace: namely, we are helpless and hopeless apart
from Christ's saving work. Each of us is spiritually
blind (John 3:3; 1 Cor. 2:14) and spiritually deaf
(John 6:43-47) apart from grace. Sinners are spiritually alienated (John 3:5; Eph. 2:11-12). We are
enslaved to the reign of sin (John 8:34) and spiritually incapacitated. Indeed, we are unable to come
to Christ apart from God's empowerment (John
6:44). Therefore, it is imperative that we resolve to
embrace a biblical understanding of sin.

2. *Resolve to Hate Sin with Holy Passion*

It is not enough to merely acknowledge the
presence, power, and penalty of sin. Thomas Watson

---

46. "Sinners in the Hands of an Angry God," in *The Works of Jonathan
Edwards*, 2 vols., ed. Edward Hickman (Edinburgh: Banner of Truth,
1974), 2:9.

spells out the severity of sin in vivid detail: "To sin still is, first, heinous, because it shows a contempt of God."[47] It is true that sin is missing the mark. But sin, in the final analysis, is a bold repudiation of God and the Word of God. Sin is a brash declaration that proclaims the radical autonomy of man and fails to recognize the distinction between the creature and the Creator.

Once we embrace a biblical understanding of sin, we are in a position to stand against it. The psalmist understands the gravity of sin and recognizes the supreme value of God's Word: "*With my whole heart I seek you; let me not wander from your commandments! I have stored up your word in my heart, that I might not sin against you*" (Ps. 119:10–11). He continues, "*Through your precepts I get understanding; therefore I hate every false way*" (Ps. 119:104). We commit our ways to God; we submit to the lordship of God; we resolve to hate sin with a holy passion.

3. Resolve to Flee From Sin

One practical result of hating sin with a holy passion is to flee from sin. When we resolve in our hearts and minds that sin is diametrically opposed to God and his ways, we will purpose in our hearts to turn from the world, the flesh, and the devil. We will flee from sin with bold resolve and trust that Christ will satisfy the deepest needs of our

---

47. Thomas Watson, *The Mischief of Sin* (Pittsburgh: Soli Deo Gloria, 1671), 54.

hearts. Instead of turning to the "filthy streams" of depravity, we will treasure Christ and drink from the crystal clear, cool, soul-satisfying streams offered in the gospel.

Joseph modeled this commitment to flee from sin when he was propositioned by Potiphar's wife in Genesis 39: *"Come lie with me,"* she demanded. *"But he refused and said to his master's wife, 'Behold, because of me my master has no concern about anything in the house, and he has put everything that he has in my charge...How then can I do this great wickedness and sin against God?'"* (vv. 8-9). Joseph wisely identified Potiphar's invitation as a "great wickedness," a word that is translated from the Hebrew term, which refers to "evil, depravity, or perversity." Potiphar's wife invited Joseph to participate in an act of evil that would rip apart her marriage and bring great dishonor to God.

Many evangelicals in our day seek to soften the severity of sin. Apparently, we are more comfortable calling adultery an "affair." Sexual sin is a "mistake" and homosexuality is an "alternative lifestyle." However, the time has come to unveil the truth about sin. The moment has arrived to speak candidly about sin and communicate its diabolical agenda. Joseph understood that succumbing to Potiphar's wife would be an act of treason against a holy God.

Potiphar's wife continued to tempt Joseph in Genesis 39. She waited for a strategic time, a time when she found Joseph working in his employer's home. He was alone and vulnerable. Verse 12 says, *"She caught him by his garment, saying 'Lie with me.'"* Once again, Joseph responded with integrity: "But he left his garment in her hand and fled and got out of the house."

Joseph's response teaches a valuable lesson that Christ-followers must emulate. Joseph made a resolution to flee from sin. Notice Joseph's bold resolve as this story unfolds. He not only identified sin as wickedness, but he acted with integrity as he literally ran away from this horrible scene. Joseph fled from sin.

So too must we flee from sin. Scripture warns, *"Flee from sexual immorality. Every other sin a person commits is outside the body, but the sexually immoral person sins against his own body"* (1 Cor. 6:18). The verb translated *flee* comes from the Greek term, *pheugō*, which means "to escape" or "avoid danger." It is a present tense imperative, reminding readers to constantly flee from sin, and in this case, sexual immorality. There is no time for sloth. Attentiveness must guard our thoughts. We must flee from sin.

But fleeing from sin is only one side of the coin. The apostle Paul utilizes the same term in 2 Timothy 2:22 when he writes, *"So flee youthful passions."* But he continues with the remainder of the imperative by grounding his thought with the word "pursue." He says, *"And pursue righteousness, faith, love, and peace, along with those who call on the Lord from a pure heart"* (2 Tim. 2:22). We are not only instructed to flee from sin, but we are called upon to strive for qualities, which are in keeping with godliness. We turn *from* sin but we turn *toward* the cross of the Lord Jesus Christ.

4. *Resolve to Admit our Sin and Confess Our Sin*

Next, we must be willing to acknowledge our sin. We have been redeemed from the *power* of sin. We have been rescued from the *penalty* of sin. And one day, we will escape the *presence* of sin. But until we escape the *presence* of sin, we continue to stand as redeemed sinners. We are *simul justus et peccator*— simultaneously righteous and sinful.

Confession of sin lies at the heart of a healthy Christian life. Romans 10:9-10 reveals that confession is necessary to receive eternal salvation: *"If you confess with your mouth that Jesus is Lord and believe in your heart that God raised him from the dead, you will be saved. For with the heart one believes and is justified, and with the mouth one confesses and is saved."* The apostle John says, *"If we say we have no sin, we deceive ourselves, and the truth is not in us. If we confess our sins, he is faithful and just to forgive us our sins and to cleanse us from all unrighteousness"* (1 John 1:8-9).

Nehemiah's prayer is instructive as he pours his heart out to God:

> *And I said, "O Lord God of heaven, the great and awesome God who keeps covenant and steadfast love with those who love him and keep his commandments, let your ear be attentive and your eyes open, to hear the prayer of your servant that I now pray before you day and*

night for the people of Israel your servants,
confessing the sins of the people of Israel,
which we have sinned against you. Even I and
my father's house have sinned. We have acted
very corruptly against you and have not kept
the commandments, the statutes, and the rules
that you commanded your servant Moses (Neh.
1:5−7).

Nehemiah is quick to confess his sin and the sins of Israel. Surely, his example is one that must be followed, especially in our day of rampant carnality. We understand that we have "an advocate with the Father, Jesus Christ the righteous" (1 John 2:2b). We don't wink at sin; we don't cover it up; we don't ignore it; and we don't "pass the buck." We strive for transparency and openness before God and man (Ps. 51:6). This kind of honesty and integrity will certainly move us in the right direction as our view of sin is reformed.

5. Resolve to Repent of All Known Sin

King David initially withheld his sin from God. Psalm 32:3 reveals the results of his hidden agenda: *"For when I kept silent, my bones wasted away through my groaning all day long. For day and night your hand was heavy upon me; my strength was dried up as by the heat of summer" (Ps. 32:4).* Yet, David came to his senses and confessed his sin to God: *"I acknowledged my sin to you, and I did not cover my iniquity; I said, "I will confess my transgressions to the LORD," and you forgave the iniquity of my sin"* (Ps. 32:5). Such confession brought health, healing, and forgiveness to the guilty king.

Before the days of the Reformation, the standard practice for a sinner involved a trip to the confessional to see a priest. The sin would be forgiven and an indulgence was granted. But God's Word clearly opposes such a practice. Sinners are called to confess and repent of all known sin to God. Such confession and biblical repentance places us on the proper path where our view of sin is being reformed.

Our View of the Gospel Must Be Reformed

Our view of God must be reformed. Our view of sin must be reformed. Finally, our view of the gospel must be reformed. Jerry Bridges writes, "The gospel is not only the most important message in all of history; it is the only essential message in all of history."[48] We must jealously guard the message of the gospel; we must maintain a biblical understanding of the gospel so that a "theological eclipse" never happens again. The gospel is our only hope for peace with God. The gospel is our only hope to be forgiven. The gospel is our only hope for eternal life (1 Cor. 15:3-5).

We must always bear in mind that the gospel is for sinners. *"And when Jesus heard it, he said to them, "Those who are well have no need of a physician, but*

---

48. Jerry Bridges, *The Discipline of Grace* (Colorado Springs: NavPress, 1994), 46.

those who are sick. I came not to call the righteous, but sinners" (Mark 2:17). Jesus came to seek and save lost people (Luke 19:10). We are numbered among the lost who have been rescued by our glorious Savior, Jesus Christ!

We must remember our offense against a holy God. We have willingly violated his holy law, the penalty of which is death (Rom. 3:23; 6:23). We can never merit favor in the eyes of a holy God. We can never work our way to a holy God. The only solution to our sin problem is to fly to the cross of Christ. Jesus died for our sins and granted forgiveness and peace to everyone who turns from their sins and trusts in him alone for salvation (Acts 4:12, 16:31; Rom. 5:1). Jerry Bridges sounds this triumphant note: "Your worst days are never so bad that you are beyond the reach of God's grace. And your best days are never so good that you are beyond the need of God's grace."[49]

THE NEED FOR REFORMATION

We are in desperate need of another reformation in the church. Once again, we see an erosion and eclipse of the gospel in our culture. We witness the rise of humanism and we observe the denial of key doctrinal propositions. We see a godless worldview, which has gained the ascendency in the public square and even in some churches.

---

49. Ibid., 18.

So bold reformers recognize the need for a new reformation. Our view of God must be reformed. Our view of sin must be reformed. And our view of the gospel must be reformed. Anything less than a reformation of truth is unacceptable for Christ-followers!

Bold reformers must resist theological compromise and respond with strength, courage, and conviction. Once our theological bearings are settled and we recognize the need for reform, we will be prepared for the next challenge. We will understand the deadly nature of compromise. And, when we have done that, we will refuse to compromise the truth.

CHAPTER THREE

BOLD REFORMERS
REFUSE TO COMPROMISE THE TRUTH

My conscience is a captive to the Word of God. I cannot and will not recant, for to disobey one's conscience is neither right nor safe. Here I stand, I cannot do otherwise. God help me. Amen.

MARTIN LUTHER,
DIET OF WORMS, APRIL 18, 1521

My grandfather, the late Rev. V.W. Steele, frequently used to say, "Never compromise the truth." "Never sell your soul for a mess of pottage," Grandpa would surmise, with fire in his eyes. He clearly understood the deadly influence of compromise. He witnessed the eroding effects of compromise, which plagued the church in his generation. He saw the crippling impact of liberalism, which waged war against the Bible and stymied the people of God. Few people listened to V.W. Steele's counsel. Ever fewer are listening today. So, compromise continues to make inroads in the lives of God's people, in the local church, and in the culture in general. A steady stream of compromise pounds relentlessly against the shoreline of the church. Unless preventative measures are taken, we will surely lose ground, which will affect the church *and* culture for generations to come.

Bold reformers refuse to compromise the truth. In this chapter, notice three emerging themes. First, *the trauma of compromise,* which looms large in our current postmodern milieu. Second, *the trial of Luther* will show how this godly reformer stood strong under fire. Third, we'll see *the traits of a man who refuses to compromise the truth.* Such a man is needed in our day, which is so characterized by compromise.

Once committed to living according to a biblical standard and seeing life through the lens of a Christ-centered worldview, compromise is rather easy to detect. The trauma of compromise makes a permanent impression and should shake a committed Christ-follower to his very core.

THE TRAUMA OF COMPROMISE

Compromise is traumatic because it wreaks havoc on individuals, the church, and the culture. "The human spirit," David Wells writes, "is now being moved not by profound thinking but by the experience of living in a metropolis presided over by bureaucracy, tranquilized by television, awash with the racket of clashing cultures."[50] Especially in our day, compromise looms large as it weasels its way into our lives and lowers biblical norms and expectations. In a recent speech, Israel's Prime Minister, Benjamin Netanyahu, warned the world of the Iranian regime and the "tentacles of terror" that threaten not only the security of Israel, but the peace and well-being of the world.[51] In like manner, the *tentacles of compromise* squeeze the life out of any willing victim. Unfortunately, these victims are often blind to those diabolical tentacles. The end result is another casualty in the church—a suffocated soul with good intentions yet rendered a spiritual weakling.

Explanation of Compromise

Compromise is a lowering of standards. It is, as the *New Oxford American Dictionary* defines it, a matter of accepting "standards that are lower than is desirable." Such a move is not in keeping with the

---

50. David F. Wells, *No Place for Truth* (Grand Rapids: Eerdmans Publishing Company, 1993), 287.
51. Mr. Netanyahu told a meeting of the American Israel Public Committee (AIPAC) that he felt compelled to speak up about the efforts to reach a deal with Iran because the "existence" of Israel is at stake. Benjamin Netanyahu, cited in David Osborne, "Netanyahu Tells AIPAC That Iran and Its International 'Tentacles of Terror' Threaten the Very Existence of Israel," *Independent*, accessed January 13, 2016, http://www.independent.co.uk/news/world/middle-east/benjamin-netanyahu-israel-faces-existential-threat-from-iran-israeli-leader-tells-aipac-10080868.html.

historic Christian faith; indeed, it is substandard. Compromise fails to honor the living God.

Compromise is a gradual erosion of what was once cherished. Typically, this deterioration is slow moving; it does not take place overnight. Rather, it is an imperceptible steady decline, which may not even be recognizable until it is too late. Like ocean waves that slowly chip away at the shores on a beautiful beach, so too does compromise gradually erode the professing Christian.

Compromise is capitulation to culture. It is a virtual surrender to the *zeitgeist*, the "spirit of the age." Paul the apostle reminded the young pastor Timothy that the last days would be marked by this kind of compromise.

> *But understand this, that in the last days there will come times of difficulty. For people will be lovers of self, lovers of money, proud, arrogant, abusive, disobedient to their parents, ungrateful, unholy, heartless, unappeasable, slanderous, without self-control, brutal, not loving good, treacherous, reckless, swollen with conceit, lovers of pleasure rather than lovers of God, having the appearance of godliness, but denying its power. Avoid such people* (2 Tim. 3:1-5).

This capitulation to culture usually takes place at a snail's pace, until one day the devastating effects reach a high point and take the unsuspecting by surprise.

Compromise is a cowardly pursuit. This mindset places higher regard for comfort and pleasure than the truth of God's Word. The sin of Samson is a tragic example of this spineless pursuit, which began in Gaza with the prostitute Delilah (Judges 16:1). Samson's disobedience cost him greatly and serves as a warning to anyone who is attracted to the things of this world, the flesh, or the devil. This cowardly pursuit may feel right initially, but it will eventually lead to a life of misery. *"Therefore the wicked will not stand in the judgment, nor sinners in the congregation of the righteous; for the LORD knows the way of the righteous, but the way of the wicked will perish"* (Ps. 1:5-6).

Compromise is ungodly. It is man-centered. It placates and caters to the flesh. It is opposed to the things of God. In our generation, compromise is viewed as a strength instead of a vice. John MacArthur adds, "Compromise has become a virtue while devotion to the truth has become offensive."[52] Compromise is viewed as a necessary and strategic move in a pluralistic society. Compromise may look right, but if left unchecked, it always leads to disaster. The Scriptures warn, *"There is a way that seems right to a man, but its end is the way to death"* (Prov. 16:25).

---

52. John F. MacArthur, *Reckless Faith: When the Church Loses Its Will to Discern* (Wheaton, IL: Crossway Books, 1994), 47.

Examples of Compromise

Compromise comes in many shapes, sizes, and colors. But make no mistake—compromise is a deadly proposition. It will annihilate pastors and elders. It will liquidate families and permanently tarnish the reputation of the most faithful man. Compromise will obliterate a church. It will tarnish a ministry. Notice a few ways this insidious disease infiltrates the local church, in particular.

A Compromised Pulpit

C.H. Spurgeon warned nineteenth-century England to steer clear from a compromised pulpit: "I do not look for any other means of converting men behind the simple preaching of the gospel and the opening of men's ears to hear it. The moment the Church of God shall despise the pulpit, God will despise her. It has been through this ministry that the Lord has always been pleased to revive and bless His churches."[53]

Luther maintained, "The pulpit is the throne for the Word of God."[54] Instead, the pulpit has become a platform for silly stories, off-color jokes, psychological tips, and man-centered "how-to's." Such a perspective shows us how far we have traveled down the path of compromise.

Al Mohler rightly says, "The health of the

---

53. Charles H. Spurgeon, *Autobiography, Volume I: The Early Years* (Carlisle: Banner of Truth Trust, 1962), v.

54. Martin Luther, cited in Steven J. Lawson, *Famine in the Land: A Passionate Call for Expository Preaching* (Chicago: Moody Publishers, 2003), 24.

church depends upon pastors who infuse their congregations with deep biblical and theological conviction, and the primary means of this transfer of conviction is the preaching of the Word of God."[55] Yet the postmodern pulpit is churning out "fast food for the soul," mere scraps which lead to spiritual malnutrition and anemia.

A compromised pulpit downplays hell and final judgment. A compromised pulpit ignores or minimizes sin and refers to depravity as a "mistake" or "error in judgment," or denies it outright. For example, Tony Jones, one of the representatives of the so-called emergent church, has stripped the doctrine of original sin from the pages of Scripture. Jones writes, "What I've come to realize is that the idea of original sin is not, in fact, God's Eternal Truth. It is, instead, like so many other items of faith, historically conditioned...I don't deny the reality of sin. But I do reject the notion that human beings are depraved from birth."[56] The repudiation of sin, hell, and final judgment will mark the end of gospel-centered preaching.

This aversion to the doctrine of original sin is shocking, yet it should come as no surprise. David Wells reports, "A majority of 52 percent of born-againers in fact reject the idea of original

---

55. R. Albert Mohler, *He is Not Silent: Preaching in a Post-Modern World* (Chicago: Moody Publishers, 2008), 111.
56. Tony Jones, *Did God Kill Jesus? Searching for Love in History's Most Famous Execution* (New York: HarperCollins Publishers, 2015), 117-118.

sin outright."[57] Wells adds, "Their way of doing church assumes the (Pelagian) view that human beings are not inherently sinful."[58] Such a view inevitably leads to a compromised pulpit which is geared to the fleshly desires of men. Man-centered preaching is merely worldliness parading about in Sunday clothes.

Compromise is desecrating the pulpit in America at an alarming rate. Hucksters promote the so-called prosperity gospel and the Word of Faith movement much to the delight of the crowds with itching ears. Compromisers step into pulpits and denigrate the authority of Scripture with man-centered rhetoric and worldly philosophy. They affirm "homosexual marriage" and assuage the conscience of people who engage in sinful activity. The level of compromise that infects the pulpit in America is unheralded and dishonors God. It must stop now!

A Compromised Theology

Compromise has led to an atrophy of theological muscle. The church, which is called to "contend for the faith" (Jude 1:3) has reached the point of cowering and, as a result, has become more comfortable with worldly ideas than the meat of the Word. Whenever sound theology is eclipsed, the result is a corruption of the truth. Relativism is

---

57. David F. Wells, *The Courage To Be Protestant* (Grand Rapids: Eerdmans Publishing Company, 2008), 57.
58. Ibid.

welcomed to a comfortable place in the center of the room. Absolute truth is left shivering out in the cold.

We live in a generation that is bored with theology. People are filled with objections to theology. Such people opine, "I'm not interested in theology." "Theological education does not work." "Tone down the message." Such statements are tantamount to a compromised theology. And a compromised theology will weaken the church and marginalize her influence in the world.

A Compromised Ecclesiology

Churches who operate according to a biblical ecclesiology, or doctrine of the New Testament church, are the exception to the rule these days. More and more churches are allowing women to fill the office of elder and even support women preaching to an audience that includes men. This move is a brazen step that jettisons the biblical imperative for male elders (1 Tim. 3:2), which prohibits women from exercising authority over a man (1 Tim. 2:11-14). The egalitarian "hooks" have been set securely, leading the church in a direction which does not honor God or the standards of his Word.

Additionally, churches are playing fast and loose by allowing unqualified men to serve in pastoral leadership roles. Only men who meet the qualifications set forth in 1 Timothy 3, Titus 1, and 1 Peter 5 are eligible to serve as elders. Measuring a man's ability to lead in the household of faith must be in alignment with God's Word. Any deviation from God's standard is destined for disaster.

A compromised ecclesiology fosters a weak leadership. Weak leadership results in a weak membership. A weak membership leads to a loss of salt and light in culture. When a church compromises her ecclesiology, everyone suffers. A compromised ecclesiology fails to honor the living God.

A Compromised Morality

Compromise has led to a loss of moral nerve in the church of Jesus Christ. For instance, a church that entertains "homosexual marriage" has a compromised morality. A church that sweeps the sin of divorce under the rug has a compromised morality. A church that ignores sexual sin has a compromised morality. This moral compromise has set the church on a trajectory that will hinder fruitful ministry and cripple her until biblical repentance takes place. God will not bless a church with a compromised morality.

These are only a few ways the church has capitulated to the spirit of the age. It is time to regain what has been lost. It is time to restore faithfulness to the local church. We must stand together as a church that refuses to compromise the truth.

THE TRIAL OF LUTHER

Martin Luther understood the paralyzing effects of compromise. He saw how compromise slithered

its way into the fabric of the church and began to
devour the gospel, verse-by-verse and line-by-line.
He witnessed how compromise in the priesthood
eroded the integrity of the church from the inside
out. Luther's pilgrimage to Rome awakened him to
the compromise that plagued the church: Martin
Marty observes, "He expressed shock at the chaos,
the filth, and the practices of locals who urinated
in public and openly patronized prostitutes."[59] He
watched with horror as the church he loved grew
more and more like the world.

Luther battled sin like every other fallen man.
Yet, he maintained a posture that served his generation well and continues to reverberate throughout the halls of church history. So Luther learned
a valuable lesson in the sixteenth century: *Bold
reformers refuse to compromise the truth.*

In 1510, Martin Luther made his first pilgrimage to Rome. His journey awakened him to the
corruption that dominated the church. He was
shocked by the carnality he witnessed among the
priesthood. The mass was conducted in a flippant
manner that horrified the young monk. Bainton
reports,

> And when he was only at the Gospel, they
> had finished and would say to him, 'Passa!
> Pass!'—'Get a move on!' The same sort
> of thing Luther could have discovered

---

59. Martin Marty, *Martin Luther: A Life* (New York: Penguin Books, 2004),
Kindle edition, Loc. 278.

in Germany if he had emerged from the cloister to visit mass priests, whose assignment it was to repeat a specified number of masses a day, not for communicants but in behalf of the dead. Such a practice lent itself to irreverence.[60]

Luther never dreamed he would experience such wanton excess and sinfulness as he made his way to the holy city: "When I first saw Rome, he recalled, "I fell to the ground, lifted my hands, and said, Hail to thee, O Holy Rome.' That impression quickly dissolved, however. He continued, 'No one can imagine the knavery, the horrible sinfulness and debauchery that are rampant in Rome.'"[61] In Luther's mind, the die was cast. And a new context emerged; a context that would set the stage for the Protestant Reformation.

THE TRAITS OF A PERSON WHO REFUSES TO COMPROMISE THE TRUTH

Like Luther, the apostles in the first century church were swimming against the cultural tide. In Acts 5, their boldness landed them in prison (v. 18). But God performed a miracle to advance his sovereign purposes: *"But during the night an angel of the Lord opened the prison doors and brought them out"* (Acts 5:19).

---

60. Bainton, *Here I Stand*, 37.
61. Luther, cited in Nichols, *Martin Luther: A Guided Tour of His Life and Thought*, 30.

God instructs these men to preach the gospel: *"Go and stand in the temple and speak to the people all the words of this Life"* (Acts 5:20). Two imperative verbs appear in verse 20. God commands the apostles to *"go"* (*poreúomai*). And God commands these men to *"speak"* (*laléō*). Both verbs are written in the present tense, which suggests ongoing action, an unceasing ministry of proclamation—despite the persecution they will continue to face.

The response of the apostles is recorded in verse 21: *"And when they heard this, they entered the temple at daybreak and began to teach. Now when the high priest came, and those who were with him, they called together the council, all the senate of the people of Israel, and sent to the prison to have them brought"* (Acts 5:21). The apostles respond with obedience, decisiveness, and bold resolve. The apostles were bold reformers!

When confronted by the officials, the response of the apostles is consistent with God's command: *"The God of our fathers raised Jesus, whom you killed by hanging him on a tree. God exalted him at his right hand as Leader and Savior, to give repentance to Israel and forgiveness of sins"* (Acts 5:30–31).

But pay close attention to the guiding principle that precedes the response of these bold reformers: *"But Peter and the apostles answered, "We must obey God rather than men"* (Acts 5:29). The Greek word translated "obey" (*peitharchéō*) means to trust or obey with confidence. That is to say, the apostles placed supreme faith in the living God, so much that they were willing to obey God from the heart. This brand of bold obedience is prepared to endure the consequences and glorify God, even to the point of death.

What are the defining features of a bold reformer who refuses to compromise the truth? What un-shakeable and unbreakable principles will guide bold reformers down a path that stands strong and steadfast before God?

1. *A bold reformer is committed to the truth of the gospel*

Bold reformers do not read the opinion polls. They do not canvas the neighborhood to see what people are interested in hearing. They do not smooth out the rough edges of the gospel in order to gain a wider hearing. They listen to God's Word; they obey God's Word; they surrender to the lordship of Christ. Bold reformers are committed to the veracity of the gospel.

2. *A bold reformer is willing to take risks for the sake of the gospel*

John Piper makes a strong case for taking risks for the sake of the gospel: "It is the will of God," writes Piper, "that we be uncertain about how life on this earth will turn out for us. And therefore it is the will of the Lord that we take risks for the cause of God."[62] Piper continues, "If our single,

---

62. John Piper, *Risk is Right: Better to Lose Your Life Than Waste It* (Wheaton, IL: Crossway Books, 2012), 30.

all-embracing passion is to make much of Christ in life and death, and if the life that magnifies him most is the life of costly love, then life is risk, and risk is right. To run from it is to waste your life."[63]

A commitment to boldness and taking risks for the sake of the gospel is a countercultural pursuit, one that will draw blank stares from some people and invite stern criticism from others. Yet, a willingness to take risks is a crucial qualification on the bold reformer's resume. Owen Strachan likewise urges Christ-followers to take risks. He writes, "We're saved to plunge headlong into a life of God-inspired, Christ-centered, gospel-driven risk. We don't know when the Master is returning; we don't know what may come of our efforts. We're not guaranteed any earthly results. But we are called to work while there still is time."[64]

So, bold reformers cut against the cultural grain. They step out in faith and trust God with the results. They go places where others fear to tread and they leave the results with God. And they may, in the final analysis, pay the ultimate price but will also reap a heavenly reward. *A bold reformer is willing to take risks for the sake of the gospel.*

* * *

63. Ibid., 17.
64. Owen Strachan, *Risky Gospel: Abandon Fear and Build Something Awesome* (Nashville: Thomas Nelson Books, 2013), 30.

The world does not need a compromised church. The compromised church will give the world what they want, not what they need. The compromised church says, "The world is tired of expository preaching." The compromised church says, "We don't exercise church discipline on the unrepentant—we just love them." The compromised church says, "Tone down the message."

The world *does* need bold reformers who refuse to compromise the truth! The world needs Christians who say what they mean and mean what they say. The world needs believers who value conviction and maintain fidelity to the Word of God. The world needs blood-bought Bible folks, people who are willing to go to any length to be numbered among the obedient. Herman Bavinck rightly identifies such a person, a theologian who bears the marks of a bold reformer: "Bound by revelation, taking seriously the confessions of the church, a theologian must appropriate the Christian faith personally. This is a liberating reality; it made it possible for heroic figures such as Martin Luther to stand up to false teaching and misconduct in the church. We must obey God rather than men."[65]

May God raise up a new generation of bold reformers who draw clear lines; people who are convinced of the truthfulness of Scripture; leaders

---

65. Herman Bavinck, *Reformed Dogmatics* (Grand Rapids: Baker Academic, 2011), 15.

who refuse to back down. This world desperately needs to hear from bold reformers who refuse to compromise the truth!

CHAPTER FOUR
BOLD REFORMERS REMAIN FOCUSED ON THE PLAN OF GOD AND THE PROMISES OF GOD

*Let goods and kindred go, this mortal life
also; The body they may kill; God's truth
abideth still; His kingdom is forever.*

"A MIGHTY FORTRESS IS OUR GOD," MARTIN LUTHER

The date was April 17, 1521. Martin Luther was summoned to appear in Worms, Germany to an event we know as the Imperial Diet at Worms. Luther was originally urged to make an appearance in Rome but avoided that trap with the help of Fredrick the Wise. Had Luther travelled to Rome, he may have never returned in one piece.

The posting of the ninety-five theses at Wittenberg managed to propel the Augustinian monk to the top of the most-wanted list. In one debate, Luther claimed that a simple schoolboy armed with the Bible was better equipped than the pope himself!

On June 15, 1520, Leo X issued a papal bull that called for the immediate restraint of the "wild boar in God's vineyard." His books were to be burned in flames and he was to be captured and sent to Rome. Luther responded to the bull in his work *On the Detestable Bull of the Antichrist*. Sixty days later, Luther burned the bull publicly in Wittenberg. He was instantly excommunicated.

When Luther arrived in Worms, he was eager for the chance to debate his Reformation ideas. Instead, he got an inquisition. As mentioned previously, two questions were hoisted upon the defrocked monk: *Are these your writings and will you recant?* He asked for one day to contemplate a proper response.

The following day, Luther made his appearance and asked for a chance to debate his ideas. The request was denied and the two questions were posed once again: *Are these your writings and will you recant?* Luther's response shook the foundations of the building and continue to reverberate through the halls of church history:

> Since then your serene majesty and your lordships seek a simple answer, I will give in this manner...Unless I am convinced by the testimony of Scripture or by clear reason, for I do not trust either in the pope or in councils alone, since it is well

known that they have often contradicted themselves, I am bound to the Scriptures I have quoted and my conscience is captive to the Word of God. I cannot and I will not retract anything, since it is neither safe nor right to go against conscience. I cannot do otherwise, here I stand. May God help me.[66]

The bold reformer was immediately placed under "imperial ban" by Charles V which meant that he could be legally hunted and killed by anyone—a piece of legislation that he lived under until the day he died.

At the conclusion of the Diet at Worms, Luther was providentially "kidnapped" by a group of bandits, secretly arranged by Fredrick the Wise. He was transported to the Wartburg Castle, which overlooks the German town of Eisenach. He was held in captivity at the castle from May 1521 to February 1522. He would sit for ten months, living under the alias *Junker Jörg*. He was a lone fugitive, an enemy of the state—living in seclusion in a cold and distant castle. No doubt, he would lie awake, wondering if a knock on the door would lead to his untimely execution. "This one monk," writes Nichols, "stood against the entire church and empire."[67] The bold reformer waited—patiently.

The fugitive did not waste any time at Wartburg,

---

66. Cited in Nichols, *Martin Luther: A Guided Tour of His Life and Thought*, 42.
67. Nichols, *Martin Luther: A Guided Tour of His Life and Thought*, 43.

however. He would spend his lonely days translating the Greek New Testament into German, a miraculous feat that he accomplished in four months.

Luther learned a practical lesson in that formidable fortress: *Whenever God's Word is on the verge of exploding, Satan works overtime.* Every time the kingdom of God expands, Satan unleashes an army of enemy combatants to militate against the people of God.

During this time, Luther experienced a raging spiritual battle. He found himself cornered in a castle. Alistair McGrath paints a vivid picture of the warfare that surrounded him: "The famous legend that Luther scared off the devil at Wartburg by throwing an inkwell at him is probably based on his statement that he had 'driven the devil away with ink,' a reference to his translation of the New Testament."[68] But the *bold reformer* endured this bitter season of spiritual warfare, which served the German people well. They were the proud recipients of a Bible translated in their own language for the first time.

Perhaps you are in a situation where you are "cornered in a castle." You feel alone; you feel attacked; you feel worn out and ready to quit the race. You understand the nature of the war; the unrelenting, unwavering battle that never seems to end. Maybe you feel anxious about the future

---

68. Alistair McGrath, *Christianity's Dangerous Idea* (New York: HarperCollins, 2007), 56.

or worried about a job interview. Perhaps you are concerned about a relationship or a troubled marriage. Or you find yourself in a ministry setting where the "house of cards" is about to collapse. Your emotions are tattered. You've burned both ends of the candle far too long. The hate mail is pouring in. People are leaving. Many, who remain, blame you for the dwindling church or organization. You're done. Game over!

The apostle Peter admonishes first-century believers in his first epistle. He admonishes Christ-followers who were "cornered in a castle." They were enduring the flames of persecution. Peter tells us about their multi-faceted experience with suffering:

- They were grieved by various trials (1 Peter 1:6).
- They were suffering for righteousness' sake (1 Peter 3:14).
- They were told not to be surprised at the fiery trial (1 Peter 4:12).
- They were admonished, "Let those who suffer according to God's will entrust their souls to a faithful Creator while doing good (1 Peter 4:19).

Life is filled with stress, anxiety, afflictions, and turmoil. Our natural tendency is to turn inward or even give up. Our regular inclination is to become self-focused. Our vision becomes myopic and often turns to self-pity. Luther refused to focus inward. He learned a crucial lesson that emerges in 1 Peter 5. In so doing, he recognized: *Bold reformers focus on the plan of God and the promises of God.* It was pivotal instruction that God would use to strengthen his resolve in the days of uncertainty and enable his hands and feet during the dark days of trial.

FOCUS ON THE PLAN OF GOD

Bold reformers focus on the three-fold plan that is unveiled in 1 Peter 5:8-9. These imperatives serve as pre-commitments for followers of Christ as they walk through the fire of adversity.

First, *be sober-minded.* This word comes from the Greek term *neiphō*—"to be calm in spirit; to demonstrate self-control."[69] The term is used throughout the New Testament (2 Tim. 4:5; 1 Pet. 1:13, 4:7; 1 Thess. 5:6, 8) and is an important first step in focusing on the plan of God. Obeying this imperative enables us to endure suffering, rely on God's grace, pray effectively, and fight the spiritual battles that God has called us to.

Second, *be watchful.* The Greek term *greigophéō* means to "stay awake; stand alert; be vigilant; beware of impending danger."[70] The term brings

---

69. James A. Swanson, *Dictionary of Biblical Languages with Semantic Domains: Greek (New Testament)* (Oak Harbor: Logos Research Systems, Inc., 1997), Logos Library System.
70. Ibid.

the image of a soldier to mind, guarding his post during the night. His mandate is clear—"Beware of the enemy! Stand guard! Be alert!"

Watchfulness and prayerfulness are viewed as companions in Scripture. For example, Jesus instructs his disciples, *"Watch and pray that you may not enter into temptation. The spirit indeed is willing, but the flesh is weak"* (Matt. 26:41). Likewise, the apostle Paul instructs the church in Colossae, *"Continue steadfastly in prayer, being watchful in it with thanksgiving"* (Col. 4:2). The masterful portrayal of the spiritual warfare that each of us face is summarized in *The Screwtape Letters* by C.S. Lewis. Screwtape (the senior demon) offers advice to Wormwood (the junior demon): "The best thing, where it is possible, is to keep the patient [the Christian] from the serious intention of praying altogether."[71] Oh, that Christians would submit to Scripture and commit themselves to watching and praying!

Watchful Christians are praying Christians. God's people are at their best when they are on their knees. Praying Christians are healthy Christians. John Bunyan adds, "Prayer is a sincere pouring out of the soul to God, through Christ, in the strength and assistance of the Holy Spirit."[72]

Are you obeying your Commanding Officer by standing your ground during a time of adversity? Are you standing watch while the enemy marches

---

71. C.S. Lewis, *The Screwtape Letters* (New York: HarperCollins, 1942), 15.

72. John Bunyan, *Prayer* (Carlisle: The Banner of Truth, 1662), 13.

through the camp? Or have you become spiritually drowsy? Has the world lulled you to sleep? Are you in a spiritual stupor? Do you find yourself "cornered in a castle?" Peter instructs believers, "Be sober-minded; be watchful."

Before we look at the third imperative, notice that Peter provides the reason for being sober-minded and watchful: *"Your adversary the devil prowls around like a roaring lion, seeking someone to devour"* (1 Pet. 5:8b). Most lions live in the Sahara desert in Africa. Imagine a roaring lion who prowls around in the desolate desert, a lion who is on a "search and destroy" mission. This is precisely the image that Peter seeks to plant firmly in our minds. No doubt, some of his first century readers saw these ferocious lions in the Roman coliseum. Some of his readers likely saw lions rip their friends to shreds!

Peter continues to describe the devil as an adversary. He is a slanderer who "inflicts persecution on believers so that they will deny Christ and lose their eschatological reward."[73] The devil is described as the serpent (Gen. 3:1; Rev. 12:9), the tempter (Matt. 4:3), the evil one (1 John 5:18-19), the prince of the demons (Mark 3:22), the Father of lies (John 8:44), a murderer (John 8:44), a thief (John 10:10), an angel of light (2 Cor. 11:14), Lucifer (Isa. 14:12), a dragon (Rev. 12:7),

---

73. Thomas Schreiner, *The New American Commentary: 1, 2 Peter, Jude*, vol. 37 (Nashville: Broadman & Holman Publishers, 2003), Logos Library System, 243.

Beelzebub (Mark 3:22), an accuser (Zech. 3:1), a deceiver (Rev. 20:7-8), and the god of this world (2 Cor. 4:4).

This vicious enemy seeks to devour followers of Christ and delivers lethal lies every day. William Gurnall adds, "The devil has more temptations than an actor has costumes for the stage. And one of his all-time favorite disguises is that of a lying spirit, to abuse your tender heart with the worst news he can deliver—that you do not really love Jesus Christ and that in your pretending, you are only deceiving yourself."[74] Gurnall summarizes the final aim of the devil: "The real goal of the devil's plot is to scare the saint and knock off the wheels of his chariot which used to carry him often into the presence of God in His ordinances."[75]

Scripture commands us to be *sober-minded* and *watchful* because this enemy prowls around like a roaring lion. We're also commanded to *resist the devil*. We're called to oppose or withstand the wiles of the devil. Scripture instructs, *"Submit yourselves therefore to God. Resist the devil, and he will flee from you"* (Jas. 4:7). In order to resist the devil, we must stand firm in the faith. In order to stand firm, we must know what we believe; that is to say, we must be grounded in sound doctrine (1 Cor. 16:13, 15:58; Eph. 6:13; Col. 2:6-7).

---

74. William Gurnall, *The Christian in Complete Armor* (Carlisle: The Banner of Truth Trust, 1655), 112.
75. Ibid.

We are commanded to resist the devil, firm in the faith, with an eternal perspective: namely, *"that the same kinds of suffering are being experienced by your brotherhood throughout the world"* (1 Pet. 5:9b). When we submit to God and resist the devil, Scripture leaves us with this promise: "he will flee from you" (Jas. 4:7).

Scripture is clear on this matter. Submit to God. Resist the devil. The devil has no choice but to flee! Martin Luther was sober-minded and watchful. And he resisted the devil, who prowled around in the Wartburg Castle. Like Luther, we too must focus on the plan of God, especially when we find ourselves cornered in a castle. As fear pounds on the castle door, we cry out with the psalmist, *"When I am afraid, I put my trust in you"* (Ps. 56:3). When worry seeks to paralyze us, we cling to the promises of God: *"Fear not, for I am with you; be not dismayed, for I am your God; I will strengthen you, I will help you, I will uphold you with my righteous right hand"* (Isa. 41:10). Every time anxiety causes our souls to shrivel, we remember the words of Jesus: *"Therefore do not be anxious about tomorrow, for tomorrow will be anxious for itself. Sufficient for the day is its own trouble"* (Matt. 6:34).

FOCUS ON THE PROMISES OF GOD

Bold reformers not only focus on the plan of God, but they also focus on the promises of God. Before Peter presents these promises, he continues to revise our perspective. He assures us this suffering will continue, albeit for a "little while." The momentary suffering we currently experience is only temporary. First Peter 5:10-11 makes it clear that our task is to focus on the promises of God.

Four Promises to Build Upon

The promises of God in Scripture are the rock-solid, soul-satisfying, blood-bought, immutable, non-negotiable words of a holy God. Like an anchor that secures a great vessel on the stormy sea, so the promises of God protect and shelter us during trials, temptations, and seasons of tribulation. The promises of God are a sure source of encouragement and stability for bold reformers who trust in his all-sufficient grace.

Peter wrote clearly to his readers in the first century. These folks were all too familiar with the theme of pain and suffering. Adversity, to these followers of Jesus Christ, was an everyday occurrence. In 1 Peter 1, the apostle reminded these dear saints of their eternal inheritance, which he described as "imperishable, undefiled, and unfading, kept in heaven for you" (v. 4). This rock-solid inheritance is *"kept in heaven"* and *"guarded through faith"* (v. 5). In light of these gospel-saturated realities, Peter encouraged them to maintain their Christian joy and eschatological, or end-time hope—despite the trials that stood before them: *"In this you rejoice, though now for a little while,*

if necessary, you have been grieved by various trials, so
that the tested genuineness of your faith—more precious
than gold that perishes though it is tested by fire—may
be found to result in praise and glory and honor at the
revelation of Jesus Christ" (vv. 6-7). Warren Wiersbe
reminds us that God sovereignly reigns over our
trials:

> When God permits his children to go
> through the furnace, he keeps his eye
> on the clock and his hand on the ther-
> mostat. If we rebel, he may have to
> reset the clock; but if we submit, he
> will not permit us to suffer one minute
> too long. The important thing is that
> we learn the lesson he wants to teach
> us and that we bring glory to him
> alone.[76]

Bold reformers have a special calling to endure
the fiery trials that come into our lives. Thankfully,
God has filled his Word with promises that will
sustain us during the difficult days and embolden
us when the flames of persecution begin. Notice
four promises that emerge in Peter's letter:

1. **He will restore us**

In the first few years of marriage, my wife and I
had an old coffee table that she decided to restore.
It was pretty beat up, so I was naturally skeptical

---

76. W. W. Wiersbe, *The Bible Exposition Commentary, Vol. 2* (Wheaton, IL:
Victor Books, 1996), 393.

about the restoration process. But she had a plan for bringing this old piece of furniture back to life again. The process was totally foreign to me as she purchased supplies that I had never heard of and engaged in a slow, tedious process to raise the old coffee table back to life. After several days of painstaking work and with the help of some good friends, she unveiled the final product. The process actually transformed an ancient coffee table into a classy piece of furniture. The coffee table was restored!

Christians too, are in desperate need of restoration. The world, the flesh, and the devil work hard to chip away at anything that resembles Christian character. The apostle John reminds us, *"For all that is in the world—the desires of the flesh and the desires of the eyes and pride in possessions—is not from the Father but is from the world"* (1 John 2:16). Add persecution to this unsavory mix, which often results in defeated and discouraged Christians. So it should come as no surprise when God promises to restore his people.

The word *restore* in 1 Peter 5:10 comes from a Greek word that means "to repair what has been broken; to restore and rehabilitate." According to Peter, Christ will render his people fit, sound, and complete. The word is used in Matthew 4:21 and Mark 1:19 in reference to "mending" nets. The same word is used in Galatians 6:1, which refers to a believer who has been been caught in a sin and is subsequently "restored" by another Christian.

God will completely restore the battered and bruised believer. He promises to repair all that has been broken. Therefore, our hope rests in the One who promises to restore us—all to the glory of God!

2. **He will confirm us**

God has blessed me with excellent health for many years. And I am grateful for the God-given strength and vitality which has enabled me to serve unhindered in ministry. However, on a few occasions, I have been afflicted with the flu. Details are not important, but I can recall losing any sign of strength, motivation, and confidence. When afflicted with an illness, basic tasks become nearly impossible.

The first-century believers were afflicted with suffering. The Greek term for suffering means "to suffer from the outside." This is a diabolical suffering, an evil affliction which is forced externally. Tom Schreiner explains this suffering:

> What Peter had in mind instead was the pattern of discrimination and abuse experienced by Christians in the Greco-Roman world. Believers stood out as social outcasts because they would not participate in any activities devoted to foreign deities and refused to live as they did formerly (1 Pet. 4:3–4). Their life as spiritual exiles explains why believers were mistreated on an informal and regular basis throughout the empire.[77]

---

77. Schreiner, *The New American Commentary: 1, 2 Peter, Jude*, 244.

So also, we are like as strangers in a strange world. We too will face inevitable persecution, persecution which is bound to intensify in the days ahead. Yet, Peter assures his readers that God will *confirm* them. The Greek term, translated *confirm*, carries the idea of strength. It means, "to be resolute." This is precisely what weak believers need as they endure these days of persecution. The terms "confirm" (*steiridzō*) and "strengthen" (*sthenóō*) which occur in 1 Peter 5:10 are similar in meaning and ultimately magnify and intensify the experience of Christians who are enabled by God to endure persecution.

3. **He will strengthen us**

Who among us cannot relate to a person in need of strength? These are difficult days that wear down the most faithful, strip courage from the most devout, and crush the hearts of diligent Christians.

Peter's original audience was all too familiar with suffering. These faithful brothers and sisters knew the sting of criticism. They were weighed down by anxious thoughts. They bore the cross of affliction. They suffered unjust persecution.

Yet God's Word makes a third promise: namely, he will *strengthen us*. The word *strengthen* is translated from the Greek word *steiridzō*. It means, "to strengthen one's soul; to set fast or fix firmly."[78] The word implies steadfastness. The same term is used in Acts 18:23, which refers to the disciples

---

78. The same word is used of Jesus when he set (*steiridzō*) his face to go to Jerusalem (Luke 9:51). Note also James 5:8 and Romans 16:25.

who were greatly *strengthened.*

The apostle Paul utilizes the term *steiridzō,* which is translated as "established" in several New Testament passages (1 Thess. 3:11-13; 2 Thess. 2:16-17, 3:3; James 5:8). Paul uses the word in Romans 1:11 to encourage the Roman believers: "For I long to see you, that I may impart to you some spiritual gift to *strengthen* you." And he uses the term *steiridzō* in his benediction to the church at Rome: *"Now to him who is able to strengthen you according to my gospel and the preaching of Jesus Christ, according to the revelation of the mystery that was kept secret for long ages" (Rom. 1:25).*

The people of God should find comfort in these precious promises, which are at their disposal. But Scripture also assures us that the God of all grace will *establish* us.

4. **He will establish us**

Circumstances are a clear and present danger as they wreak havoc on devoted followers of Christ. External persecution dominates the marketplace of ideas and internal persecution batters the church. Worldly philosophy and cultural pressure abound. Social media and Madison Avenue compete for the hearts and minds of young people. The entertainment industry demands unceasing attention and devotion. There are a myriad of ideologies, isms, and worldviews that pose a pernicious brand of pressure and which threaten the foundation of Christ-followers.

But Peter sets forth a final promise in verse 10: namely, God will establish us. The word is *themelióō,* which means "to lay the foundation; to cause to be steadfast." The same word is used in Colossians 1:23. The apostle Paul writes, "...If indeed you continue in the faith, *stable (themelióō)* and steadfast, not shifting from the hope of the gospel that you heard, which has been proclaimed in all creation under heaven, and of which I, Paul, became a minister."

Here is the promise of almighty God: he promises *himself*—the God of all grace—that he will "restore, confirm, strengthen, and establish us." He allows persecution and adversity to work their way into our lives, which ultimately produce Christian character. *"Not only that, but we rejoice in our sufferings, knowing that suffering produces endurance, and endurance produces character, and character produces hope"* (Rom. 5:3–4). "God's consistent purpose, during whatever times of exile and disappointment he takes you through, is to prepare you for future service and a deepened appreciation of his grace."[79] God stands behind all our suffering and will use it to strengthen us, conform us to the image of his Son, and bring him great glory! Rooted and grounded in him, God will empower us to endure in the midst of any circumstances.

---

79. Iain Duguid, *Living in the Grip of Relentless Grace* (Phillipsburgh, PA: P & R Publishing, 2015), Kindle edition, Loc. 960.

REMAINING FOCUSED ON THE RIGHT THINGS

Luther was penned up in the Wartburg castle for nearly ten months. It is vitally important to understand his response. He refused to get passive. He declined to become self-focused and feel sorry for himself. Rather, he used these days of bitter providence to translate the Greek New Testament in German, the common language of the people. The result—his work fueled the fires of the Protestant Reformation!

When the people of God are backed into a corner, important ministry takes place, significant accomplishments are achieved, people are evangelized, books are written, and fruit is produced to the glory of God! And Luther is not the only one who accomplished great things when his back was against the wall. Christian leaders in the halls of church history have engaged in God-honoring ministry through difficult times that we still continue to benefit from today:

- John Bunyan penned *Pilgrim's Progress* in prison.
- William Cowper wrote amazing hymns during bouts with depression.
- C.H. Spurgeon preached powerful sermons despite his struggle with depression.
- Jonathan Edwards wrote some of his most important works after he was fired from his church in Northampton.

Is your back against the wall? Are you facing the flames of persecution? Do you feel like throwing in the towel? Do you find yourself "cornered in a castle?" Oh, bold reformer, God calls you to focus on his plan and focus on his promises—*"to him be the dominion forever and ever. Amen"* (1 Pet. 5:11). May you trust his sweet plan and believe his precious promises. And may you rest in the sovereignty of God. This is the next great theme toward which we turn our attention.

CHAPTER FIVE

BOLD REFORMERS
REST IN THE SOVEREIGNTY OF GOD

That word above all earthly powers,
no thanks to them, abideth;
the Spirit and the gift are ours, thru him who with us sideth.
Let goods and kindred go, this mortal life also;
the body they may kill; God's truth abideth still;
his kingdom is forever.

"A MIGHTY FORTRESS IS OUR GOD,"
MARTIN LUTHER

We have seen the great benefit of focusing on the plans of God and the promises of God. Indeed, a life of faith will gravitate toward all that he has planned and all that he promises to do. We have observed how steadfast and unwavering commitment help embolden God's people—even as they walk through the flames of adversity and endure the furnace of persecution.

This chapter argues that bold reformers must also rest in the sovereignty of God. Resting in the sovereignty of God is an act of faith. Such faith is rare in our generation. A Christ-entranced faith is marginalized by the unbelieving world and frowned upon in a culture that rests in and relies on the idol of human ingenuity. To cast our hope upon the unseen is viewed with suspicion and is scorned by the erudite.

But this kind of audacious faith is essential for bold reformers who fear God above all and trust him implicitly. The author of Hebrews reminds us, *"And without faith it is impossible to please him, for whoever would draw near to God must believe that he exists and that he rewards those who seek him"* (Heb. 11:6). Faith is a prerequisite for resting in the sovereignty of God. Thomas Watson remarks, "Faith believes the promise; but that which faith rests upon in the promise is the person of Christ."[80] Therefore, we abandon the disintegrating "scaffolding" of human ingenuity and bank our hope on God's ability to work for us. We rest in the sovereignty of God.

Luther Rested in the Sovereignty of God

It is easy to idealize men like Luther and set aside their sins and struggles. Luther was a sinner

---

80. Thomas Watson, *A Body of Divinity* (Carlisle: The Banner of Truth Trust, 1692), 216.

like anyone else and wrestled fervently with in-
dwelling sin. He battled pride. He waged war with
a temper that posed problems on the battlefield. He
uttered words that were not befitting of a Christian
man. Yet, this sinful man rested in the sovereignty
of God.

It is no secret that Luther battled fear and
anxiety, an ailment sometimes referred to as
spiritual depression.[81] Luther referred to these
bouts of spiritual depression as *anfechtungen*. The
German term is difficult to translate but has the
connotation of being "under assault." The word is
closely associated with "temptation" or "despair."
It has connotations with what is typically referred
to as "the dark night of the soul." Luther even
considered penning a book about *anfechtungen*. His
interest in *anfechtungen* was driven, of course, by
several personal experiences throughout his life.

Wager with God

The first noticeable experience with *anfechtungen* came in Luther's so-called *wager with God*.
As related earlier, after completing his graduate
work in 1505, he was cut to the quick as he faced
a turbulent thunderstorm. Fearing death, he was
compelled to cry out, "Help me, St. Anne, and I
will become a monk." Of course, he made good
on his promise as he entered the Augustinian

---

81. For a thorough treatment, see Martyn Lloyd-Jones, *Spiritual Depression*
(Grand Rapids: Eerdmans Publishing Company, 1965).

monastery in 1506. This providential event forced him to experience *anfechtungen* at an early age and would have a profound influence on his life, not to mention the trajectory of church history.

Worship Service

Luther's next experience with *anfechtungen* took place at a *worship service*. Lifting his hands to the heavens, as he presided over his first Mass, the young monk froze. In a moment of time he was stricken with a deep sense of *anfechtungen*. "I am dust and ashes and full of sin," the junior monk lamented. Roland Bainton captures the spirit of that dread-filled day: "Toward God he was at once attracted and repelled. Only in harmony with the Ultimate could he find peace. But how could a pigmy stand before divine Majesty; how could a transgressor confront divine Holiness?"[82] Once again, Luther faced the terrifying experience of *anfechtungen*.

Wariness Before God

Sometime in 1516, the German monk began to experience a nagging *wariness before God*. Luther cried out, "Sometimes Christ seems to me nothing more than an angry judge who comes to me with a sword in his hand."[83] He was tormented by his inability to please a holy God. He virtually drove his

---

82. Bainton, *Here I Stand*, 31.
83. Martin Luther, cited in Sproul, *The Holiness of God*, 75.

mentor Johann Von Staupitz crazy as he struggled spiritually and questioned how he could ever merit favor before God. "How can a sinful man stand in the presence of a holy God?" Questions like this haunted Luther and drove him to Scripture for the answer where he was confronted by the truth of justification by faith alone in Romans 1:16-17. These vexing questions not only affected Luther's spiritual and emotional health; they affected his physical health as well. He was plagued by fits of sweating, despair, and heart palpitations. He was convinced that if he should breathe his last, he would be ushered promptly to the gates of hell!

Wittenberg

Luther's conversion prompted a new set of convictions that eventually led him to a public debate. On October 31, 1517, he posted his famous ninety-five theses and was no doubt immediately confronted with *anfechtungen* at Wittenberg. *Who would read his theses? What kind of controversy would they bring?* Such troubling questions would culminate in a whole new set of circumstances that the reformer would be forced to address. Little did Luther know that his act of boldness would change the world!

Worms

Worms was Luther's next significant experience with *anfechtungen* as he stood before the authorities of the Roman Catholic Church. As noted earlier, Luther was asked whether the books spread out before him were his. "Will you recant?" was the cry that echoed in his ears. At first, he hesitated. After weighing the options before him, Luther uttered the words that would reverberate around the world as an act of boldness:

> Since then your serene majesty and your lordships seek a simple answer, I will give it in this manner, plain and unvarnished: Unless I am convinced by the testimony of the Scriptures or by clear reason, for I do not trust either in the pope or in councils alone, since it is well known that they often err and contradict themselves, I am bound to the Scriptures I have quoted and my conscience is captive to the Word of   God. I cannot and I will not retract anything, since it is neither safe nor right to go against conscience. I cannot do otherwise. Here I stand. May God help me, Amen.[84]

While troubled with another round of *anfechtungen*, the bold reformer was taking shape.

Wartburg Castle

After the troubling scene at the Diet of Worms, Luther was whisked away by his friend Fredrick the Wise as described in chapter one. Surely, the bold reformer faced fears on several fronts as he braved the chilly halls of the Wartburg castle.

---

84. Martin Luther, cited in Nichols, *The Reformation: How a Monk and a Mallet Changed the World*, 32.

Surely, he battled the dreaded *anfechtungen* during these troubling times. Yet the bold reformer kept his gaze on the cross work of the Savior. In all his weakness, the bold reformer was drawing strength from Christ. Perhaps the words of the apostle comforted him in these days of seclusion: *"For the sake of Christ, then, I am content with weaknesses, insults, hardships, persecutions, and calamities. For when I am weak, then I am strong"* (2 Cor. 12:10).

His Truth to Triumph Through Us

Martyn Lloyd-Jones maintains, "The ultimate cause of all spiritual depression is unbelief."[85] Of course, Luther was not the only well-known figure in church history to battle with spiritual depression. It is a well-known fact that some of the greatest Christian minds struggled with intense bouts of melancholy.

Jonathan Edwards was overly introspective which became a detriment in ministry. William Cowper fought feelings of suicide for most of his adult life. Prior to his conversion, Cowper lamented, "Day and night I was upon the rack, lying down in horror, and rising up in despair."[86] Readers who wonder if Cowper's battle with depression vanished after he was miraculously converted will be disappointed.

---

85. Martyn Lloyd-Jones, *Spiritual Depression* (Grand Rapids: Eerdmans Publishing Company, 1965), 20.
86. Gilbert Thomas, *William Cowper and the Eighteenth Century* (London: Ivor Nicholson and Watson, Ltd., 1935), 204, cited in John Piper, *The Hidden Smile of God* (Wheaton, IL: Crossway Books, 2001), 84.

John Piper reveals, "William Cowper's life seems to be one long accumulation of pain."[87] Such pain often extends beyond the miracle of regeneration and inflicts faithful followers of the Lord Jesus Christ.

And C.H. Spurgeon trudged through the slough of despondence for most of his ministry. In a letter to his mother, Spurgeon writes, "In the blackest darkness I resolved that, if I never had another ray of comfort, and even if I was everlastingly lost, yet I would love Jesus, and endeavor to run in the way of his commandments: from the time I was enabled thus to resolve, all these clouds have fled."[88] Even the prince of preachers battled this vexing unbelief.

Lloyd-Jones concludes, "The main art in the matter of spiritual living is to know how to handle yourself...You must turn on yourself, upbraid yourself, condemn yourself, exhort yourself, and say to yourself: 'Hope thou in God'—instead of muttering in this depressed unhappy way."[89] As Christians, we are called to demolish strongholds and take every thought captive to Christ (2 Cor. 10:5). We are admonished in Scripture to present our bodies to God—as a living sacrifice, to be

---

87. John Piper, *The Hidden Smile of God* (Wheaton, IL: Crossway Books, 2001), 90.
88. C.H. Spurgeon, cited in Tom Nettles, *Living By Revealed Truth: The Life and Pastoral Theology of Charles Haddon Spurgeon* (Geanies House, Scotland: Christian Focus Publications, 2013), 53.
89. Lloyd-Jones, *Spiritual Depression*, 21.

transformed by the renewing of our minds (Rom. 12:1-2). Philippians 4:4-6 says, "*Rejoice in the Lord always; again I will say, rejoice. Let your reasonableness be known to everyone. The Lord is at hand; do not be anxious about anything, but in everything by prayer and supplication with thanksgiving let your requests be made known to God.*"

Clearly, many Christ-followers battle spiritual depression. Lloyd-Jones urges,

> You must go on to remind yourself of God, Who God is, and what God is and what God has done, and what God has pledged himself to do. Then having done that, end on this great note: defy yourself, and defy other people, and defy the devil and the whole world, and say with [the psalmist]: "I shall praise Him for the help of His countenance, who is also the health of my countenance and my God."[90]

But what about Martin Luther? How did he battle his fear, anxiety, and despondency? How did he face the dread of *anfechtungen?* Several lines from his famous hymn *A Mighty Fortress is Our God* provide clues that give us an initial idea of how Luther battled this formidable foe:

For still our ancient foe
Doth seek to work us woe
His craft and pow'r are great

---

90. Ibid.

And, armed with cruel hate
On earth is not his equal
And though this world with devils filled
Should threaten to undo us
We will not fear for God hath willed
His truth to triumph thru us

The prince of darkness grim
We tremble not for him
His rage we can endure
For lo, his doom is sure
One little word shall fell him

Luther was quick to acknowledge the spiritual battle he faced. But he was also ready to wage war by using God's appointed means. We turn our attention to one of the chief ways that Luther battled the dark nights of *anfechtungen*.

Bold reformers rest in the sovereignty of God. Notice two crucial tools in Luther's arsenal: tools available to every follower of Jesus Christ.

TURN TO THE SOVEREIGN LORD

"I lift up my eyes to the hills. From where
does my help come?
My help comes from the LORD, who made
heaven and earth."
(Ps. 121:1-2)

The Scriptures present a God who is sovereign over all things. His sovereignty has no limits and knows no bounds. The sovereignty of God is absolute and comprehensive. James Boice describes this sovereign God: "He has absolute authority and rule over his creation. In order to be sovereign, God must also be all-knowing, all-powerful and absolutely free. If he were limited in any one of these areas, he would not be entirely sovereign."[91] Our sovereign King reigns over all the earth!

Psalm 121 models what it means for a sinful person to turn to the sovereign LORD. In the Old Testament, God's people would make their way to Jerusalem for the annual feasts. Since there were no real roads to speak of in those days, it is easy to see how this psalm would have provided deep encouragement for the weary Jewish traveler. Imagine making the long journey to the holy city. Your bones ache. Your throat is parched. Fear is your constant companion. And suddenly, you cast your eyes upon the hills of Judah: *"I lift my eyes to the hills. From where does my help come from? My help comes from the LORD, who made the heaven and the earth" (Ps. 121:1-2).*

C.H. Spurgeon captures the flavor of such a faith-filled look: "The purposes of God; the divine attributes; the immutable promises; the covenant, ordered in all things and sure; the providence, predestination, and proved faithfulness of the Lord— these are the hills to which we must lift up our eyes, and from these our help must come."[92] It is to

91. James Boice, *The Sovereign God* (Downers Grove: InterVarsity Press, 1978), 149-150.
92. C.H. Spurgeon, *The Treasury of David, Volume 3* (Peabody: Hendrickson Publishers), 14.

this God that we direct our attention. We turn to the sovereign LORD.

We shall see that turning to the sovereign LORD is an important act of faith. It is not only an act of faith; it is an act of obedience. Notice several important components of a person who turns to this sovereign king.

A Heart that is Riveted on God

Turning to the LORD requires a heart that is focused on God. *"I lift up my eyes to the hills. From where does my help come from?" (Ps. 121:1).* Such a heart is captivated by the beauty of the Creator. When our hearts are concentrating on God, it pre-supposes proactivity. It involves patient discipline. Gazing in God's direction is never an accidental endeavor. Rather, the one who is directed toward this sovereign God looks to him with intentionality. This look acknowledges need. This, indeed, is a look of faith.

A Heart That Runs to God

A heart that turns to the LORD will, by definition, pursue God. There is a holy longing after God that saturates the heart of a person who is truly seeking the LORD. Deuteronomy 4:29 is a snapshot of the one who runs to God: *"But from there you will seek the Lord your God and you will find him, if you search after him with all your heart and with all your soul."* And 2 Chronicles 7:14 captures the essence of a person who runs to God: *"If my people*

who are called by my name humble themselves, and pray
and seek my face and turn from their wicked ways, then
I will hear from heaven and will forgive their sin and
heal their land." Such is the man whose heart chases
after God.

A Heart That Remembers the Creator

A heart that turns to the LORD is quick to acknowledge God is the Creator. A brief survey of
Scripture reminds us that God is the Creator of
all things (Isa. 42:5; Ps. 124:8; Col. 1:15-16; Acts
17:24). Acknowledging that God is the Creator
is a necessary prerequisite for turning to him.
Establishing that God is the Creator reminds us
that we are the creatures. The so-called Creator-
creature distinction is an important aspect of
building our Christian worldview. Peter Jones
writes, "The starting point of Gospel truth is that
God the Creator, in the three persons of the Divine
Trinity—Father, Son, and Holy Spirit—is the one
and only God, and that all which is not God was
created by him."[93]

The Creator-creature distinction reminds us that
God is in charge. He calls the shots. He is sovereign
over all that he created. Therefore, the creatures
are obligated to submit to his kingly authority. The
creatures are bound to obey the commands of the
Creator, without hesitation. Anything that falls

---

93. Peter Jones, *Gospel Truth/Pagan Lies* (Enumclaw, WA: Main Entry Edi-
tions, 1999), 24.

short of obedience to God is tantamount to cosmic treason.

The Creator-creature distinction reminds us of the infinite chasm that exists between the Creator God and his creation. This worldview is opposed to the panentheistic notion promoted by thinkers like Doug Pagitt. In his book, *Flipped: The Provocative Truth That Changes Everything We Know About God*, Pagitt argues, "All that exists is in God."[94] The author adds, "God is not a separate subject that we talk about or relate to through belief, behavior, faith, or practice. Much better than that, God is the very existence of all things."[95] Such a notion does violence to the Creator-creature distinction and is filled with theological difficulties.

Scripture presents a God who is distinct from his creation *and* distinct from his creatures. The panentheistic model celebrates the immanence of God while minimizing the supreme transcendence of God. However, Scripture presents a God who is altogether transcendent *and* immanent. Isaiah 57:15 shows how God's transcendence and immanence are simultaneous realities that we must embrace if we are to worship God rightly: *"For thus says the One who is high and lifted up, who inhabits eternity, whose name is Holy: 'I dwell in the high and holy place, and also with him who is of a contrite and lowly spirit, to*

---

94. Doug Pagitt, *Flipped: The Provocative Truth That Changes Everything We Know About God* (Convergent Books, 2015), Kindle edition, Loc. 223.
95. Ibid., Loc. 229.

revive the spirit of the lowly, and to revive the heart of the contrite.'" We do violence to the sovereign God of the universe when we fail to acknowledge both his transcendence and his immanence.

A Heart That Rejoices in the Sustainer

Finally, every heart that turns to the LORD must rejoice in the Sustainer. God's Word clearly shows how Jesus, the second member of the Trinity, sustains all things:

> *And he is before all things, and in him all things hold together* (Col. 1:17).

> *He is the radiance of the glory of God and the exact imprint of his nature, and he upholds the universe by the word of his power. After making purification for sins, he sat down at the right hand of the Majesty on high* (Heb. 1:3).

Since Jesus sustains all things by the word of his power, we can be assured that we live in an ordered universe.

So, bold reformers turn to the sovereign LORD. Our hearts are riveted on God. Our hearts run to God. We remember our Creator. And we rejoice in our God who sustains all things by the word of his power. However, not everyone turns to the LORD. Those who refuse to turn to the LORD act according to their strongest inclination—they turn away from him.

All who turn from the LORD are governed and

imprisoned by pride. Proud people are autono-
mous. They place confidence in their own abilities.
Proud people trust themselves and they do not have
time for God or his Word. An example of such a
man is Nebuchadnezzar. Instead of displaying the
regal majesty of a king, Nebuchadnezzar had more
in common with a mad man, a lunatic on the verge
of insanity. Scripture says that God stripped him
of the kingdom and sent him to pasture where he
scavenged in the field like an animal. His finger-
nails grew like the claws of a bird. But in a twist of
providential favor, God restored the sanity of the
king: *"At the end of the days I, Nebuchadnezzar, lifted
my eyes to heaven, and my reason returned to me, and I
blessed the Most High, and praised and honored him who
lives forever, for his dominion is an everlasting dominion,
and his kingdom endures from generation to generation"*
(Dan. 4:34).

The consequence of pride is a sobering reality.
God's Word teaches that pride comes before a fall
(Prov. 16:18). Pride discounts God (Prov. 10:4).
Pride is numbered among the sins that God hates
(Prov. 8:13). The proud man cannot stand in God's
presence (Isa. 2:17). And the proud person is
opposed by God—for *"God opposes the proud but gives
grace to the humble"* (Jas. 4:6).

Where then, shall we go when we are at the end
of our rope? Certainly, resisting God and proudly
refusing his leadership in our lives is not the path
we wish to follow. We follow the lead, then, of the
psalmist and *turn to the LORD*. And in so doing, our

hearts will be riveted on God. Our hearts will run to God. But, the Scriptures also beckon us to *trust in the sovereign LORD.*

TRUST IN THE SOVEREIGN LORD

"He will not let your foot be moved; he who keeps you will not slumber. Behold, he who keeps Israel will neither slumber nor sleep. The LORD is your keeper; the LORD is your shade on your right hand. The sun shall not strike you by day, nor the moon by night. The LORD will keep you from all evil; he will keep your life. The LORD will keep your going out and your coming in from this time forth and forevermore."
(Ps. 121:3-8)

God not only created the heaven and the earth (Ps. 121:2), but he also sustains and controls them. Our God governs all things for his glory (Col. 1:16-17; Heb. 1:3). Therefore, we trust in the LORD, who is in providential control of all things. The Westminster Confession of Faith is of immense help on this matter:

God the great Creator of all things doth uphold, direct, dispose, and govern all creatures, actions, and things, from the greatest even to the least, by his most wise and holy providence, according to his infallible foreknowledge, and

*the free and immutable counsel of his own
will, to the praise of the glory of his wisdom,
justice, goodness, and mercy.*[96]

Bold reformers understand that God exercises
comprehensive control over all things. Thus, the
notion of "fate" or "chance" is not a part of their
vocabulary. Indeed, such a notion is a pagan idea.
Proverbs 21:1 affirms that God is sovereign over all
things—even in the heart of a world leader: *"The
king's heart is a stream of water in the hand of the LORD;
he turns it wherever he will."* God's control over all
things extends to the actions of the creatures and
every event in the natural world (Prov. 19:21; Job
37:9-13). Ephesians 1:11 affirms, *"In him we have
obtained an inheritance, having been predestined according
to the purpose of him who works all things according to
the counsel of his will."* That is to say, the ultimate
end culminates in the glory of God (Rom. 11:36).

Divine Protection

In Psalm 121:3-8, the word *keep* occurs six
times. The psalmist obviously had a specific reason
for using this word, which means "to watch over,
guard, preserve, secure, or protect."

God providentially protects his people. One
commentator reveals, "God, who watches over his
own, will not slumber or sleep, that is, he will not
be indifferent to or disregard them. The Lord will

---

96. G.I. Williamson, ed. *The Westminster Confession of Faith* (Phillipsburg,
PA: Presbyterian & Reformed, 1964), 60.

be alert in protecting his own."[97] God providentially provides for the needs of his people (vv. 4-6). Notice the comprehensive nature of this help—"*the sun shall not strike you by day, nor the moon by night.*" God providentially protects his people from evil (v. 7). And verse 8 contains a wonderful summary statement which includes a mighty promise: *he providentially protects* his *people and provides for* his *people.*

During the most difficult years of my most recent pastorate, there were days when the false accusations were flying. My character was being attacked on a regular basis. People who didn't know any better believed the lies. They cherished the gossip. The bitter fruit blossomed and left me cold, disillusioned, and discouraged. God calls us, however, to rest in his sovereignty.

Turning to the LORD and trusting the LORD are marks of a God-centered faith, faith that treasures Christ above all and believes the promises of God. These are important qualities of a bold reformer. A bold reformer turns to the LORD and trusts in the LORD: namely, the bold reformer rests in the sovereignty of God.

Bold reformers do well to remember four important principles when the days become especially difficult and discouraging:

97. A.P. Ross, *Psalms*, in J.F. Walvoord & R.B. Zuck, eds., *The Bible Knowledge Commentary: An Exposition of the Scriptures* (Wheaton, IL: Victor Books, 1985), 1:833.

1. **Absolutely nothing can touch our lives without God's permission.**

In Job 1, God permits Satan to afflict Job: *And the LORD said to Satan, "Behold, all that he has is in your hand. Only against him do not stretch out your hand"* (Job 1:12a).

In Job 2, the LORD clears the path for Satan to afflict Job: *"And the LORD said to Satan, "Behold, he is in your hand; only spare his life"* (Job 2:6). In both instances, God sets the parameters of suffering and stands behind this suffering. That is to say, God is in control of both the scope and the extent of all our suffering.

In Luke 22:31, the devil is on the prowl for another man. This time he wants to sink his satanic claws into Peter: *"Simon, Simon, behold, Satan demanded to have you, that he might sift you like wheat"* (Luke 22:31). Peter would later write to believers, *"Be so-ber-minded; be watchful. Your adversary the devil prowls around like a roaring lion, seeking someone to devour"* (1 Pet. 5:8). The phrase, *sift like wheat* comes from the Greek term *siniádzō*, which means, "to shake violently or agitate the faith of someone with the intention of destruction." But notice the prayer of Jesus in the next verse: *"but I have prayed for you that your faith may not fail. And when you have turned again, strengthen your brothers"* (Luke 22:32).

There is an unshakeable contrast that emerges between Job and Peter. Job does *not* deny God. Peter *does* deny his Lord. Yet God preserves the salvation of both men. Peter fails but his faith is not overthrown. Remember that Christ prayed for him, that his faith might not fail. Peter's trial has a refining effect on his life. He refers to this lesson in 1 Peter 1:6-7: "*In this you rejoice, though now for a little while, if necessary, you have been grieved by various trials, so that the tested genuineness of your faith—more precious than gold that perishes though it is tested by fire—may be found to result in praise and glory and honor at the revelation of Jesus Christ.*"

So God sets the parameters of suffering. Nothing can touch God's people without God's permission. His purposes, even in the midst of pain and suffering, are good. Indeed, his purposes are meant for our good and to magnify the greatness of his worth.

The apostle Paul reminds us, "*Who shall separate us from the love of Christ? Shall tribulation, or distress, or persecution, or famine, or nakedness, or danger, or sword? As it is written, 'For your sake we are being killed all the day long; we are regarded as sheep to be slaughtered.' No, in all these things we are more than conquerors through him who loved us. For I am sure that neither death nor life, nor angels nor rulers, nor things present nor things to come, nor powers, nor height nor depth, nor anything else in all creation, will be able to separate us from the love of God in Christ Jesus our Lord*" (Rom. 8:35–39).

2. God's sovereign control over all things extinguishes our fear.

Psalm 56:3-4 says, "*When I am afraid, I put my trust in you. In God, whose word I praise, in God I trust;*

I shall not be afraid. What can flesh do to me?" God's sovereign control over all things reminds us that when faith reigns, fear is powerless. When faith rules, fear is erased. Oh, that we would turn again and again to the doctrine of God's sovereignty which extinguishes our fear.

3. **God's sovereign control over all things builds our faith.**

Recognition of God's sovereignty can only help, sustain, and build our faith when we face seasons of doubt, adversity, trial, and suffering. Spurgeon is quick to remind us:

> I believe that every particle of dust that dances in the sunbeam does not move an atom more or less than God wishes—that every particle of spray that dashes against the steamboat has its orbit, as well as the sun in the heavens—that the chaff from the hand of the winnower is steered as the star in their courses. The creeping of an aphid over the rosebud is as fixed as the march of the devastating pestilence—the fall of leaves from a poplar is as fully ordained as the tumbling of an avalanche.[98]

Affirming God's sovereign control over all things puts everything in proper perspective as we roll our problems on the One who sees the end from

---

98. C.H. Spurgeon, *God's Providence in Spurgeon Sermons* (Grand Rapids: Baker Books, 1883), 201.

the beginning. Our triune God governs the most tyrannical world leader (Prov. 21:1). He governs the weather patterns and controls every tsunami, earthquake, and hurricane (Ps. 147:16-18). He even gathers the casting of lots (Prov. 16:33). Indeed, our triune God governs all things: *"In him we have obtained an inheritance, having been predestined according to the purpose of him who works all things according to the counsel of his will"* (Eph. 1:11).

4. When we trust in the promises of God, he is greatly glorified.

The Bible is filled with God's promises which are directly focused on his people for their well-being. Hebrews 11:1 reminds us, *"Now faith is the assurance of things hoped for, the conviction of things not seen."* In verse 6, we are admonished to be a people of faith: *"And without faith it is impossible to please him, for whoever would draw near to God must believe that he exists and that he rewards those who seek him"* (Heb. 11:6). God is greatly glorified as we bank on his promises and cast our hope and future on him.

"ABSOLUTE SOVEREIGNTY IS WHAT I LOVE TO ASCRIBE TO GOD"

Resting in the sovereignty of God is a steep learning curve for most people. As a young man, Jonathan Edwards battled the doctrine of God's sovereignty with all his might. He confesses, "From my childhood up, my mind had been full of objections against the doctrine of God's sovereignty...It used to appear like a horrible doctrine to me."[99] Edwards was, in the final analysis, forced to love the doctrine of God's sovereignty or utterly reject it. Listen to the radical shift that takes place in his heart: "There has been a wonderful alteration in my mind, in respect to the doctrine of God's sovereignty...The doctrine has very often appeared exceeding pleasant, bright, and sweet. Absolute sovereignty is what I love to ascribe to God."[100]

Martin Luther was a man who rested in the sovereignty of almighty God. This bold reformer not only taught about the sovereignty of God, he breathed it and lived it. Luther's faith in God's sovereign control over all things is clearly revealed in Wittenberg, Worms, the Wartburg Castle and beyond. May bold reformers in this generation draw strength and courage from the life and legacy of Luther, a man who rested in the sovereignty of God.

---

99. Jonathan Edwards, "Personal Narrative," cited in John Piper, *Desiring God* (Sisters: Multnomah Books, 1996), 39.
100. Ibid., 40.

CHAPTER SIX
BOLD REFORMERS
REJOICE IN THE HOPE OF THE GOSPEL

For God has not destined us for wrath, but to obtain salvation through our Lord Jesus Christ, who died for us so that whether we are awake or asleep we might live with him. Therefore encourage one another and build one another up, just as you are doing.

1 THESSALONIANS 5:9–11

One of the most fundamental truths in Scripture is this: *He saved us* (Tit. 3:5; Matt. 1:21). First Thessalonians 5 introduces the biblical reality of "the day of the Lord" (v. 2), that time when "God will visit the world to bring this age to its end and to inaugurate the age to come."[101] Whether Christ's

---

101. George Ladd, *A Theology of the New Testament* (Grand Rapids: Eerdmans Publishing Company, 1974), 600.

return comes before the Great Tribulation, in the midst of the Great Tribulation or after the Great Tribulation—this fact remains: The second coming of Christ should motivate us to be alert and live in the light (1 Thess. 1:4-8).

These are important things to consider. For we live in an age where fear surrounds us—the threats of terrorism, nuclear war, cancer, Alzheimer's disease, economic collapse, and unemployment. The prospect of such things has the power to shake a person to the core. But the Word of God should shape our perspective, not circumstances or current events.

So, Paul the apostle provides motivation for believers who are assaulted with fear. He not only instructs us to be alert and live in the light, but he also sets forth our final destiny and spells out the hope that we enjoy as Christians. The unwavering hope of every bold reformer is found in the amazing reality that Jesus saved his people from their sins. Therefore, bold reformers rejoice in the hope of the gospel.

SAVED FROM THE WRATH OF GOD

We must come to terms with what we have been delivered from: namely, the wrath of God. Jonathan Edwards describes wrath as the just punishment which sin deserves: "Sin against God, being a violation of infinite obligations, must be a crime infinitely heinous, and so deserving infinite punishment."[102] Understanding the wrath of God, then, is of critical importance for the bold reformer.

Understanding the Wrath of God

The wrath of God is his indignation and anger displayed in the punishment of sinners. Notice how three godly men describe the wrath of God:

> The wrath of God is his eternal detestation of all unrighteousness...It is the holiness of God stirred into activity against sin... God is angry against sin because it is a rebelling against his authority, a wrong done to his inviolable sovereignty.[103]

> [God's wrath] is his steady, unrelenting, unremitting, uncompromising antagonism to evil in all its forms and manifestations.[104]

> The bow of God's wrath is bent and the arrow made ready on the string, and justice bends the arrow at your heart and strains the bow; and it is nothing but the mere pleasure of God, and that of an angry God, without any promise or obligation at all, that keeps the arrow one moment from being made drunk with your blood.[105]

---

102. *The Works of Jonathan Edwards*, vol. 1, *The Justice of God and the Damnation of Sinners*, ed. Edward Hickman (Carlisle: The Banner of Truth Trust, 1834), 669.

103. A.W. Tozer, *The Attributes of God* (Grand Rapids: Baker Book House, 1975), 83.

104. John Stott, *The Cross of Christ* (Downers Grove: InterVarsity Press, 1986), 173.

105. *The Works of Jonathan Edwards*, vol. 1, *Sinners in the Hands of an Angry God*, ed. Edward Hickman (Carlisle: The Banner of Truth Trust, 1834), 9.

The wrath of God is clearly seen in the Old Testament (Isa. 13:13; Jer. 30:23-24; Isa. 30:27-33; Lev. 10:1-3; 2 Sam. 6:1-7). Yet, some scholars seek to confine the wrath of God to the Old Testament exclusively. One writer says, "In the teaching of Jesus, anger as an attitude of God to men disappears, and his love and mercy become all embracing."[106] But the wrath of God is clearly seen in the New Testament as well (Matt. 3:7; John 3:36; Rom. 1:18, 2:5; Col. 3:5).

The focus, however, is on the hope of every follower of Christ. Disciples of Jesus Christ are not destined for wrath. Paul notes, "For God has not destined us for wrath" (1 Thess. 5:9a). The word *destined* means to "set into place; to fix, establish, ordain; to render or appoint." The term appears at numerous points throughout the New Testament and is translated in various ways:

- God *fixes* times (Acts 1:7).

- God *appoints* his people to bear fruit (John 15:16).

- He *made* you overseers (Acts 20:28).

- God *appoints* believers to salvation (1 Thess. 5:9).

This is the hope of every Christ-follower. God has not destined us for wrath. We have been saved

---

106. C.H. Dodd, cited in Leon Morris, *The Apostolic Preaching of the Cross* (Grand Rapids: Eerdmans Publishing Company, 1955), 179.

from the wrath of God. We have escaped a horrible and infinite punishment. But our destiny involves more than merely escaping the wrath of God. We are saved *through* the Son of God.

SAVED THROUGH THE SON OF GOD

Paul continues to encourage the Thessalonians and every subsequent follower of Christ: *"For God has not destined us for wrath, but to obtain salvation through our Lord Jesus Christ, who died for us"* (1 Thess. 5:9-10a).

Marveling at the Death of Christ

God has not destined us for wrath as we saw in verse 9. Rather, we have been predestined to obtain salvation. The word translated *obtain* comes from a Greek word which means "to acquire or purchase." The word has the connotation of "enjoyment as well as acquisition." The same word is translated as *"the purchased possession"* (Eph. 1:14), *"a people for his own possession"* (1 Pet. 2:9), and *"obtain the glory of our Lord Jesus Christ"* (2 Thess. 2:14).

Our salvation is wrapped up in four words: *Christ died for us.* In Romans, Paul articulates the horrifying reality of the curse: that we are sinners who have transgressed the law of God (Rom. 3:23); that we are hardened sinners with a passion for selfishness and disobedience (Rom. 3:5, 8); that *"all have sinned and fall short of the glory of God"* (Rom. 3:23). Indeed, we are sinners by nature and by choice. But in Romans 5, Paul magnifies the grace of God in this monumental sentence, which has eternal implications for every believer: *"But God shows his love for us in that while we were still sinners, Christ died for us"* (Rom. 5:8).

This is the truth that we must marvel at. This is the truth that should captivate our minds and melt our hearts: *Christ died for us!* It is a horrifying reality that Jesus bled on the cross and bore the sin of every person who would ever believe. But Christ's death on the cross is also the most beautiful event in all of human history. On the cross of Christ, mercy and justice meet! This work is summarized in the doctrine of substitutionary atonement— what theologians refer to as penal substitution.

The atonement is *penal* in that Christ bore the penalty for our sins. It is *substitutionary* in that Christ took the place of sinners. He stood in our place. Please note a few crucial features of penal substitutionary atonement.

Jesus stands in as our substitute. Hebrews 9:26 says, *"For then he would have had to suffer repeatedly since the foundation of the world. But as it is, he has appeared once for all at the end of the ages to put away sin by the sacrifice of himself."* Jesus bore the wrath we deserved.

Jesus reconciles us to a holy God. This ministry of reconciliation is necessary since we are enemies of God and separated from him because of our sin. Scripture reminds us, "But your iniquities have made a separation between you and your God, and your sins have hidden his face from you so that he does not hear" (Isa. 59:2). Paul the apostle sounds this high note to the Colossian church: "And you, who once were alienated and hostile in mind, doing evil deeds, he has now reconciled in his body of flesh by his death, in order to present you holy and blameless and above reproach before him" (Col. 1:21-22).

Jesus redeems us from our sin. Redemption is necessary since we are slaves to sin—hopeless and helpless (John 8:34). Sinners are bound to their sin; they are utterly enslaved to this brutal task-master. Paul triumphs in Jesus' redeeming work as he spells out this magnificent ministry to the Ephesians: "*In him we have redemption through his blood, the forgiveness of our trespasses, according to the riches of his grace*" (Eph. 1:7).

Finally, *Jesus is our propitiation.* We deserve the wrath of God. We deserve the judgment of God. We stand guilty before a holy God. In the New Testament we find that God himself provides the means of removing his wrath (1 John 4:10; 1 John 2:2; Rom. 3:25). Jesus Christ is our propitiation as he satisfies the righteous demands of the law. Indeed, Jesus affirms the love of God and absorbs the white-hot wrath of God the Father. We are saved *from* the wrath of God. We are saved *through* the Son of God. And we marvel at the death of Christ.

SAVED FOR THE GLORY OF GOD

Our goal, of course, is to live for Christ and to live for his glory. Paul's passion for the Christian life runs throughout the New Testament:

- "So whether we are at home or away, we make it our aim to please him" (2 Cor. 5:9).

- We "walk in a manner worthy of the Lord" (Col. 1:10).

- We "walk in a manner worthy of the calling to which you have been called" (Eph. 4:1).

- "So whether you eat or drink, or whatever you do, do all to the glory of God" (1 Cor. 10:31).

And Paul writes in 1 Thessalonians 5:10, *"Whether we are awake or asleep we might live with him."* The Greek word translated *live* means "to be strong; to be efficient; to be full of life and vigor; to be powerful." Matthew Henry comments, "On the contrary, Christ died for us, that, living and dying, we might be his; that we might live to him while we are here, and live with him when we go hence.[107] Bold reformers are saved for the glory of God!

---

107. Matthew Henry, *Matthew Henry's Commentary on the Whole Bible: Complete and Unabridged in One Volume* (Peabody: Hendrickson, 1994), 2344.

THE UNSHAKEABLE HOPE OF BOLD REFORMERS

We have an unshakeable hope because we are saved from the wrath of God and saved through the Son of God. These realities give rise to a new way of living. These realities spark a new set of motivations. These gospel truths propel us into the future and enable us to live our lives to the glory of God!

So as bold reformers, we live to the glory of God in every sphere of our lives. Our unshakeable hope enables us to live to the glory of God:

- In the office

- At the mill

- Selling a product

- Repairing a car

- Riding a bicycle

- Playing an instrument

- Working with patients

- Raising children

- Delivering a package

- Dealing with controversy

- Planning for the future

- Making an arrest

- Defending a client

- Fixing a computer

- Preaching a sermon

- Teaching a class

Bold reformers are saved from the wrath of God, through the Son of God, in order to live to the glory of God. "*So, whether you eat or drink, or whatever you do, do all to the glory of God*" (1 Cor. 10:31). Paul concludes his argument in verse 11 with practical encouragement: "*Therefore encourage one another and build one another up, just as you are doing.*"

How can bold reformers be of encouragement to other followers of Christ? Note three concluding principles: first, *we should keep reminding each other about these truths.* The word *encourage* means "to console" or "come alongside." It means to "comfort the person who struggles with doubt." The word is a present tense verb, which means the ministry of encouragement should be a daily habit for every bold reformer. Additionally, the word is written in the imperative mood. So encouraging others is not an option—it is a command! The same word appears several times in the New Testament. One shining example appears in Acts 14:22 where we find bold reformers who are committed to encouraging their fellow disciples to stand firm in the faith (Acts 14:22). Paul sent Tychicus to the

Colossian believers for the specific purpose of encouragement (Col. 4:7-8). We too are called upon to encourage one another in the Christian faith.

Second, *comfort the weak with the truth of the cross.* Paul's challenge to the Thessalonians is to "*build one another up.*" The word comes from the Greek term *oikodomeō*, which means "to build a house; construct or restore a building; and to promote growth in Christian virtues such as wisdom, affection, virtue, holiness, and grace." It is also written in the present tense and imperative mood. So building one another up is a command to be obeying on a daily basis! The best way to build people up is to direct their attention to the cross work of the Lord Jesus Christ. Point them to the cross. Direct them to their place of deliverance. Build them up by reminding them that they have been saved from the penalty of sin and the power of sin. And one day, they shall be free from the presence of sin.

Third, *we should constantly remind each other about our position in Christ.* Remind them about the truth of 1 Thessalonians 5:9-11. Remind them about their hope in Christ. We have been saved from the wrath of God. We have been saved through the Son of God. We are saved so that we might live to the glory of God. Bold reformers rejoice in the hope of the gospel!

If you are not a Christ-follower, your destiny is an altogether different proposition. Without the grace of God, you will face the wrath of almighty God. Without the grace of God you will stand before the Son of God and face his eternal judgment. "You must either fear his future wrath, or love his present grace—one of the two."[108]

So, bold reformers turn their attention to the cross of Christ—the same cross that Luther wrote about and preached about. Bold reformers are comforted by the truth of the cross. They are challenged by the demands of the cross and they are humbled at the foot of the cross. When the world flees from the cross, the bold reformer returns to the cross on a daily basis.

Bold reformers must stand together. We must maintain our ground as we bank all our hope in the gospel. We must stand strong and rest in all that Christ has accomplished. We must point to the glory of the cross again and again. For only at the cross do we find forgiveness and freedom in Christ alone. Indeed, bold reformers rejoice in the hope of the gospel!

---

108. Ignatitus, cited in Colin Brown, *Dictionary of New Testament Theology* (Grand Rapids: Zondervan Publishing House, 1967), 112.

CHAPTER SEVEN
BOLD REFORMERS
RESOLVE TO PROCLAIM THE GOSPEL

Him we proclaim, warning everyone and teaching everyone with all wisdom, that we may present everyone mature in Christ.

COLOSSIANS 1:28

Christians who dare to make a bold stand will face opposition. Any Christian leader who dares to preach dogmatic doctrinal propositions and draw bold lines in the sand is bound to end up in hot water somewhere along the line. Bold reformers resolve to proclaim the gospel. They proclaim the gospel faithfully and courageously and rely on the power of the Holy Spirit to bring a fruitful harvest.

BOLD REFORMERS PROCLAIM A STRONG MESSAGE

We live in an age where anyone who dares to stand up as a bold reformer is met with suspicion and skepticism. But, living in postmodern times should not deter bold reformers from faithfully proclaiming the Word of God. Paul the apostle instructs the believers in Colossae: *"Him we proclaim, warning everyone and teaching everyone with all wisdom, that we may present everyone mature in Christ"* (Col. 1:28). The ministry that Paul demands here involves *strong proclamation* that refuses to waver, despite the reaction from the culture at large. The Greek verb *kataggello* means, "to declare plainly, openly, and aloud; to announce, to celebrate, to preach." In Acts 17:2-3, we find Paul engaged in the ministry that he demands from the Colossian believers: *"And Paul went in, as was his custom, and on three Sabbath days he reasoned with them from the Scriptures, explaining and proving that it was necessary for the Christ to suffer and to rise from the dead, and saying, 'This Jesus, whom I proclaim to you, is the Christ'"* (Acts 17:2–3). J. I. Packer refers to the gospel as "a proclamation of divine sovereignty in mercy and judgment, a summons to bow down and worship the mighty Lord on whom man depends for all good...Its center of reference was unambiguously God."[109] Notice several features of strong proclamation:

---

109. Introductory essay by J.I. Packer in John Owen, *The Death of Death in the Death of Christ* (Carlisle: The Banner of Truth Trust, 1684), 2.

1. **Strong proclamation must be Christ-centered**

Christ-centered preaching does not soften the hard edges of the gospel. This kind of preaching staunchly resists the health and wealth "gospel." Preaching that is Christ-centered refuses to elevate man's free will. And Christ-centered preaching refuses to minimize God's sovereignty. Christ-centered preaching must be gospel preaching; preaching that proclaims that Jesus died for sinners and was raised for our justification (Rom. 4:25); preaching that proclaims sinners may be forgiven (Acts 13:48); preaching that proclaims the way of salvation (Acts 16:17). Packer adds, "The preacher's task...is to display Christ: to explain man's need of him, his sufficiency to save, and his offer of himself in the promises as Savior to all who truly turn to him; and to show as fully and plainly as he can how these truths apply to the congregation before him." Strong proclamation must be Christ-centered.

2. **Strong proclamation must be unabashedly bold**

Christ-centered proclamation, by definition, must exalt Christ and will lead to bold proclamation. Jonathan Edwards makes this case clear in his sermon *Christ the Great Example of Gospel Ministers:*

> They should imitate [Christ] in the manner of his preaching; who taught not as the scribes, but with authority, boldly,

zealously and fervently; insisting chiefly on the most important things in religion, being much in warning men of the danger of damnation, setting forth the greatness of the future misery of the ungodly; insisting not only on the outward, but also the inward and spiritual duties of religion; being much in declaring the great provocation and danger of spiritual pride, and a self-righteous disposition; yet much insisting on the necessity and importance of inherent holiness, and the practice of piety.[110]

Paul modeled this bold proclamation in his preaching ministry: "This I *proclaim* to you" (Acts 17:23ff). This is the battle cry of the bold reformer! He commits himself to bold proclamation. *"For I am not ashamed of the gospel, for it is the power of God for salvation to everyone who believes"* (Rom. 1:16).

Additionally, they "shall guard the pulpit by ensuring that sound doctrine is proclaimed faithfully and boldly; doctrine which does not deviate from the *Sola Scriptura* principle."[111] Timid proclamation is tantamount to cowardice and has no place among bold reformers.

---

110. Wilson H. Kimmach, *The Works of Jonathan Edwards, Christ the Great Example of Gospel Ministers* (New Haven: Yale University Press, 2006), 339.
111. Christ Fellowship Statement of Faith & Corporate By-Laws, Revised 2015.

3. Strong proclamation must be fearless

Of course, we live in a cowardly culture, where many preachers capitulate and compromise the precious doctrinal realities of Scripture. We can scarcely recall the days of the Puritans when the doctrines of hell, unconditional election, the sovereignty of God, the ministry of the Holy Spirit, and the lordship of Christ were powerfully proclaimed from their pulpits. Paul the apostle "did not shrink" from declaring the truth of God's Word (Acts 20:20). Bold reformers should do no less. We must wield the mighty sword by the power of the Spirit.

4. Strong proclamation must be comprehensive

Strong proclamation must include the whole of Scripture. Bold reformers must resist the urge to present the Bible in bits and pieces: "For I did not shrink from declaring to you the whole counsel of God" (Acts 20:27). Therefore, the *only* way and the most effective way of proclaiming the Scripture in a comprehensive way is expository preaching. Any other method will inevitably fall short and will leave the people of God malnourished.

5. Strong proclamation must lay the foundation for the Christian worldview

I will never forget the beginning stages of construction on Safeco Field in Seattle, Washington. Huge pillars were relentlessly pounded into the ground to ensure a solid, stable, and safe structure.

Likewise, strong proclamation must lay the foundation for the Christian worldview which includes the following concepts. Bold reformers must drive home the reality that Christ is at the center of all things. The Scripture tells us that Christ is the creator of all things (Col. 1:16), Christ is the sustainer of all things (Col. 1:17), Christ is the Redeemer of sinful men (Col. 1:13-14), and Christ will make all things new (Rev. 21:5). So, bold reformers have a responsibility to present the Christian worldview. This will strengthen believers *and* challenge the pagan presuppositions of an unbelieving world.

6. Strong proclamation must carry the full weight of biblical authority

Strong proclamation must reprove, rebuke, exhort, and include solid teaching in keeping with 2 Timothy 4:1-4. So, bold reformers preach a strong message, a message that carries the full weight of biblical authority. They must confront worldly ideology (Col. 2:8). Lloyd-Jones referred to preaching as "logic on fire." Therefore, bold reformers are faced with the challenge of presenting the weighty truths of Scripture with passion and God-centered logic.

7. Strong proclamation must have a sense of urgency

Strong proclamation must be blood-earnest and have a sense of gravitas. Bold reformers must say what they mean and mean what they say. Paul the apostle adds, "*Therefore be alert, remembering that for three years I did not cease night or day to admonish every one with tears*" (Acts 20:31). Boring preaching should be considered a capital crime. Woe to the preacher who puts his people asleep. The preaching of the bold reformer must alert sinners and challenge the saints. It must beckon sinners to come to the cross and break their pride. The preaching of the bold reformer must have a sense of urgency!

8. Strong proclamation must be intensely theological

Al Mohler rightly says, "As a theologian, the pastor must be known for what he teaches as well as what he knows, affirms, and believes. The health of the church depends upon pastors who infuse their congregations with deep biblical and theological conviction, and the primary means of this transfer of conviction is the preaching of the Word of God."[112] Consequently, theological categories should be taught relentlessly for the building up of the body of Christ.

9. Strong proclamation must make a lasting difference in the hearts and minds of people

Lloyd-Jones writes, "Preaching should make such a difference to a man who is listening that

---

112. R. Albert Mohler, *He is Not Silent: Preaching in a Postmodern World* (Chicago: Moody Publishers, 2008), 111.

he is never the same again."[113] Luther's tireless work and faithful proclamation made a difference in the lives of the German people, not to mention the continent of Europe. His strong proclamation made a lasting difference in the hearts and minds of people. Likewise, our messages must be a catalyst to transform believers into fruitful disciples of Christ.

So, strong proclamation matters for the bold reformer. These things matter deeply. May the courage and conviction of the "wild boar in the vineyard" capture the hearts and minds of pastors and Christian leaders all around the world. And may they proclaim the message of the gospel so the nations might rest and rely on the all-sufficient Savior, the Lord Jesus Christ! May they stand among the bold reformers who faithfully wield the mighty Word of God!

BOLD REFORMERS PROVIDE A SERIOUS WARNING

Bold reformers not only proclaim a strong message; they warn people with this message. Notice how Paul spells out his argument in Colossians 1:28. *"Him we proclaim, warning everyone and teaching everyone with all wisdom, that we may present everyone mature in Christ."*

---

113. Martyn Lloyd-Jones, *Preaching and Preachers* (New York: HarperCollins, 2012), 53.

The ministry of warning is a key component in repertoire of every bold reformer. The Greek word *noutheteō,* translated as "warning" in this passage, means "to admonish, instruct, exhort, or warn." One commentator adds, "Admonishing in Scripture has the connotation of confronting with the intent of changing one's attitudes and actions."[114] The term addresses the task of calling to mind a correct course of action.

Bold reformers consistently *warn people about the lure of sin* (Jas. 1:14-15; Prov. 4:14-15). They *warn people to flee from idolatry* (1 John 5:21; 1 Cor. 6:18; Heb. 12:14). Bold reformers *warn people about the end result of unbelief* (Rom. 2:5; Heb. 3:12). And bold reformers *warn everyone.* John MacArthur remarks, "If there is sin in the life of a believer, other believers have the responsibility to lovingly, gently admonish them to forsake that sin."[115] Scripture adds, *"I myself am satisfied about you, my brothers, that you yourself are full of goodness, filled with all knowledge and able to instruct (noutheteō) one another"* (Rom. 15:14).

---

114. Richard R. Melick, *The New American Commentary: Philippians, Colossians, Philemon,* vol. 32 (Nashville: Broadman & Holman Publishers, 2001), Logos Library System.
115. John F. MacArthur, *Colossians and Philemon* (Chicago: Moody Publishers, 1992), 79.

BOLD REFORMERS PRESENT SYSTEMATIC TEACHING

Bold reformers understand that proclaiming Christ involves strong proclamation and serious, soul-shaking warning. But it involves a third component: namely, systematic teaching.

1. He proudly intends to put the church on display

The Greek word, *paristēmi* is translated as the English term *present*. It is an aorist tense verb and implies that this "presentation" will occur in the final eschatological day. The image brings a class of college students to mind who are *presented* at a graduation, displayed on stage and recognized for their accomplishments, having labored over their studies. The students are presented publicly and conferred with a reward—a degree. The aim here is to "present everyone mature in Christ."

2. He aims to see people mature in Christ

Paul refers to the *telos* or the goal of God's elect: *"And those whom he predestined he also called, and those whom he called he also justified, and those whom he justified he also glorified" (Rom. 8:30).* It is a fascinating thing to see the Greek word for maturity emerge in Colossians 1:28, a word which is translated "maturity" and means, "full-grown or complete."

Until we all attain to the unity of the faith and of the knowledge of the Son of God, to **mature** *(teleios) manhood, to the measure of the stature of the fullness of Christ* (Eph. 4:13).

Epaphras, who is one of you, a servant of Christ Jesus, greets you, always struggling on your behalf in his prayers, that you may stand **mature** *(teleios) and fully assured in all the will of God* (Col. 4:12).

This is the intention of the apostle. Indeed, this is the intention of every bold reformer.

A PLEA FOR BOLD PROCLAMATION

We have seen that the time is ripe for a new reformation. Now is the time for bold reformers to make their mark on the world for Jesus Christ. But one final plea is in order. This is a plea of God-centeredness, a radical pursuit of God in all his glory. Such is the life of a bold reformer. Our prayer is that these marks of maturity would be revealed in at least three areas.

1. **A God-centered view of God**

A.W. Tozer summarizes this mark of maturity in his classic *The Knowledge of the Holy*: "What comes into our minds when we think about God is the most important thing about us...So necessary to the church is a lofty concept of God that when that concept in any measure declines, the church with her worship and her moral standards declines along with it."[116] Tozer understood the importance of God-centeredness. And he understood the dire consequences for people and churches who compromise the doctrine of God. He adds, "The first step down for any church is taken when it surrenders its high opinion of God."[117]

We have a propensity to distort the vision of God presented in Scripture.[118] We downplay his authority; we soft-peddle his sovereignty. In an effort to emphasize his immanence, we neglect his transcendence. And in an effort to emphasize his transcendence, we minimize his immanence. Both views are wrongheaded and lead to tragic theological errors. Most notably, these errors have massive epistemological implications. John Frame reminds us,

> The unbiblical form of transcendence leads to epistemological irrationalism, and the unbiblical form of immanence leads to rationalism. But it is plain in the biblical narrative that, contrary to irrationalism, God and his truth can be known, for he has revealed himself clearly to us (Rom. 1:19-20). And contrary to rationalism, autonomous reasoning is foolishness (Prov. 3:5-8; 1 Cor. 1:20-30).[119]

---

116. Tozer, *The Knowledge of the Holy*, 1, 4.
117. Ibid., 4.
118. The best-selling book *The Shack* by William Young is a classic example.
119. John M. Frame, *Systematic Theology: An Introduction to Christian Belief*

Simply put, "God does not lower his standards to accommodate us."[120] So bold reformers make it their aim to serve, love, and worship the God who is presented in sacred Scripture. The bold reformer has a God-centered view of God.

2. A God-centered view of the church

Calvin argued that a true church rightly preaches the Word of God, faithfully administers the ordinances and takes church discipline seriously. May God help any body of believers who compromises in any of these areas. Additionally, Paul told Timothy *"how to behave in the household of God, which is the church of the living God, a pillar and buttress of the truth"* (1 Tim. 3:15).

Tragically, the church is drowning in a sea of pragmatism, pluralism, relativism, and compromise. The church is being assaulted by worldliness, both internally and externally. The schemes of men are popular. The ancient creeds are being cast aside. Deep theological roots are being systematically pulled up, and the church is growing weaker by the day. Now is the time for the people of God to make their mark. Now is the moment for men and women of God to stand tall and proclaim the doctrines of grace with vigor and vitality. Now is the time for faithful proclamation. Now is the time for truth. Indeed, the bold reformer has a God-centered view of the church.

(Phillipsburg, PA: Presbyterian and Reformed, 2013), 57.
120. Sproul, *The Holiness of God*, 88.

3. A God-centered view of the gospel

Spurgeon notes,

> I do not believe we can preach the gospel...unless we preach the sovereignty of God in his dispensation of grace; nor unless we exalt the electing, unchangeable, eternal, immutable, conquering love of Jehovah; nor do I think we can preach the gospel unless we base it upon the special and particular redemption of his elect and chosen people which Christ wrought out upon the Cross; nor can I comprehend a gospel which lets saints fall away after they are called.[121]

The prince of preachers rightly highlights the importance of a God-centered view of the gospel, a gospel that clearly articulates the doctrines of grace, a gospel that is Calvinistic, a gospel that glorifies God alone!

This is the same gospel that Jonathan Edwards preached in Northampton, the very gospel that Calvin preached in Geneva. This is the identical gospel that Luther preached in Germany. Spurgeon adds,

> The old truth that Calvin preached, that Augustine preached, is truth that I must preach today, or else be false to my conscience and my God. I cannot shape the truth; I know of no such thing as paring off the rough edges of a doctrine. John

---

121. Spurgeon, *Autobiography: Volume 1, The Early Years*, 172.

Knox's gospel is my gospel. That which thundered through Scotland must thunder through England again.[122]

This gospel is for sinners like you and me. If you understand that you have offended a holy God; that you have committed cosmic treason; that you have violated his law and that the sword of judgment could fall any moment at your feet—please understand that there is a solution to this perplexing problem. Fly to the cross of Christ. Jesus died for sinners so they might have peace with God and be forgiven of all their sin (Acts 4:12, 16:31). Your answer is found in Christ alone.

Bold reformers understand the gospel implicitly. They understand that sinners are dead in trespasses and sins (Eph. 2:1-3). They acknowledge that sinners can't lift a finger for God apart from grace. Bold reformers marvel in grace; they revel in grace; they delight in grace. And they sing with the hymn writer:

Long my imprisoned spirit lay
Fast bound in sin and nature's night:
Thine eye diffused a quickening ray;
I woke; the dungeon flamed with light;
My chains fell off, my heart was free:
I rose, went forth, and followed Thee.[123]

---

122. Ibid., 162.
123. Charles Wesley, "And Can It Be?"

GOD-CENTERED PROCLAMATION

Do you have a God-centered view of God? Do you have a God-centered view of the church and a God-centered view of the gospel? Bold reformers are relentlessly God-centered in the way they conduct their lives. Paul the apostle was a bold reformer in this sense. His words to the Colossians cannot be more clear: *"Him we proclaim, warning everyone and teaching everyone with all wisdom, that we may present everyone mature in Christ"* (Col. 1:28).

Like every bold reformer, Paul resolved to make a stand for the gospel. His heart was to proclaim Christ for a purpose: namely, to present everyone mature in Christ. May this passion and purpose dominate your life. May the resolution to stand firm for the gospel consume your thoughts and dreams. May this commitment influence your pocketbook. And may this gospel-saturated resolution fuel your resolve for the nations to find their joy in Christ.

My prayer is that God will mercifully raise up a new generation of bold reformers who make their mark on this generation. May bold reformers make a stand for the gospel in the marketplace of ideas—cities and villages—and in the academy, boardroom, athletic fields, shopping centers, and parks. Oh, that bold reformers would step into pulpits with fresh determination to stand strong for the gospel and raise the banner of truth for the sake of the nations. May bold reformers proclaim Christ with power and precision so that people may be presented mature in Christ!

CHAPTER EIGHT
BOLD REFORMERS
REMEMBER TO STAND FIRM IN THE GOSPEL

As good stewards, we must maintain the cause of truth against all comers. 'Never get into religious contro- versies,' says one; that is to say, being interpreted, 'Be a Christian soldier, but let your sword rust in its scabbard, and sneak into Heaven like a coward.' Such advice I cannot endorse. If God has called you by the truth, maintain the truth which has been the means of your salvation. We are not to be pugnacious, always contending for every crotchet of our own; but wherein we have learned the truth of the Holy Spirit, we are not tamely to see that standard torn down which our fathers upheld at the period of their lives. This is an age in which truth must be maintained zealously, vehe- mently, continually. Playing fast and loose, as many do, believing this today and that tomorrow, is the sure mark of children of wrath; but having received the truth, to hold fast the very form of it, as Paul bid Timothy to do, is one of the duties of heirs of Heaven. Stand fast for truth, and may God give the victory to the faithful.[124]

C.H. SPURGEON

We have seen an example of an extraordinary man—Martin Luther—who has earned the title *bold reformer*. Among other things, we have observed a person who:

- Recognized the need for reform

- Refused to compromise the truth

- Remained focused on the plan of God and the power of God

- Rested in the sovereignty of God

- Rejoiced in the hope of the gospel

- Resolved to proclaim the gospel

Luther has given us an example to follow when the storms of life threaten to blow us away. He has offered us a role model to emulate when discouragement strikes or false accusations fly, and he has displayed remarkable courage in the face of overwhelming adversity. Martin Luther has exemplified these things for the glory of God. Indeed, he was a bold reformer.

---

124. Spurgeon, *Autobiography: Volume 1, The Early Years*, 470.

One characteristic remains, however, which encompasses all of what we have seen thus far. Without this final quality, we become vulnerable. Without this essential trait, we are at risk and will soon be banished to the sidelines. The ultimate mark of the bold reformer is this: *he remembers to stand firm in the gospel.*

Scripture recounts several cases where men of God stood firm and resolute for the glory of God:

- Noah stood firm despite the mocking crowd around him.

- Moses stood firm despite the diabolical schemes of the pharaoh.

- Joseph stood firm despite the wicked actions of his brothers and Potiphar's wife.

- Joshua stood firm despite the rebels who surrounded him.

- Nehemiah stood firm despite the nitpicking crowd who mocked and belittled him.

- Job stood firm despite a wife who pleaded with him to *curse God and die.*

- Samuel stood firm despite a nation who compromised and a king who capitulated.

- Josiah stood firm despite the compromise perpetuated by the culture and other kings.

- Isaiah stood firm despite the military invasion of the enemies of God.

- Jeremiah and Ezekiel stood firm despite the rampant idolatry that surrounded them.

- Daniel stood firm despite an empire who opposed the plans and purposes of a holy God.

- Amos stood firm despite the corruption and the apostasy that plagued his culture.

- Micah stood firm despite the crooked men who oppressed the poor.

- John the Baptist stood firm and endured a horrible death to the glory of God.

- The apostle Paul stood firm despite weaknesses, insults, hardships, persecutions, and calamities.

- Jesus Christ stood firm despite being tempted in all ways as we are, yet remained without sin, and endured the cross to the glory of God.

THE CALL

In 2011, I submitted my resignation to a church I loved. I had served as pastor of theology for over eleven years and had experienced the honor of ministering with Pastor Wayne Pickens, a godly man with a heart for people and an uncompromising commitment to Scripture. While Wayne and I endured many challenges in this church, our commitment to one another and our passion for serving the church never faltered. Wayne patiently nurtured me, pointed out "blind spots," and gave me the freedom to exercise my gifts in ministry. It was a relationship built on mutual trust. Those days at First Baptist in La Grande made a permanent impression on me and forever marked my approach to life and pastoral ministry.

My tenure at First Baptist came to a screeching halt as I accepted the call to serve as senior pastor at a new church in late 2011. The transition was difficult, to say the least, as we moved to a different community and a new church family.

After serving two years, a bitter split led over one hundred people away from the new church I pastored, leading to a season of discouragement, fear, and anxiety for me. I remember a *watershed meeting* with a trusted friend from another church who gave me some wise and godly counsel. I asked him, "Why do you think God called me here?" Clearly, it was a loaded question, but my friend answered without missing a beat: "God called you to this church to stand firm," he said. He continued to breathe strength into my soul as the wisdom poured from his mouth. But it was the words "stand firm" which continued to surface in my mind. These words remained with me for the rest of the evening. They remained with me for the rest of the week. And they continue to encourage me to this day.

The call to stand firm is clearly taught in Scripture. Several sections of the New Testament mark out the path for bold reformers. These passages are dripping with perseverance. They help us understand the importance of standing firm and persevering in the truth of the gospel. Doing so means we stand firm for orthodoxy and the historic Christian faith. Bold reformers refuse to waver in their beliefs. We stand with Paul the apostle who challenged the Ephesian believers to *"attain to the unity of the faith and of the knowledge of the Son of God, to mature manhood, to the measure of the stature of the fullness of Christ, so that we may no longer be children, tossed to and fro by the waves and carried about by every wind of doctrine"* (Eph. 4:13-14). Rather, we are grounded in biblical theology and systematic theology. We are entrenched in the gospel. Therefore, we remember to stand firm in the gospel, and Scripture urges us to stand firm in several ways:

Be Watchful

Bold reformers are called upon to *stand watch*. First Corinthians 16:13 helps define the call on the life of every bold reformer: *"Be watchful, stand firm in the faith, act like men, be strong."*

The Greek verb, translated *watchful*, means to "stay awake; stand alert; be aware of danger; stand vigilantly." This imperative warns us to steer clear from spiritual drowsiness. Several years ago, I began taking a natural herb called *melatonin*. This little pill helps me fall asleep and usually makes me drowsy just prior to dosing off. But in the Christian

life, we are warned against spiritual drowsiness
(Matt. 26:38, 41; Col. 4:2; 1 Pet. 5:8; Acts 20:31).
There is an alarming trend of "spiritual sleep-
iness" among evangelicals in the church today,
especially men. Frankly, many men have checked
out. Some Christian men are "asleep at the wheel."
Instead of being watchful and alert, they allow
ungodly influences to infiltrate their families.
They allow ungodly influences to penetrate their
churches. Like a night watchman who falls asleep
and allows thieves and robbers to ransack the
fortress, disaster hovers menacingly as Christian
men are asleep in the night.

We have a propensity to grow lazy in the Christian
life. It is so easy to let things slide. The imperative
to remain *watchful* helps prevent spiritual sloth. It
helps prevent spiritual drowsiness. It provides an
incentive for Christian leaders to stand ready, to
defend the truth and declare the truth.

Standing watch is crucial for at least three
reasons. First, *we must be watchful to avoid being taken
captive.* God's Word warns us, *"See to it that no one
takes you captive by philosophy and empty deceit, according
to human tradition, according to the elemental spirits
of the world, and not according to Christ"* (Col. 2:8).
Remaining watchful helps prevent being dragged
into the ideological camp of the enemy.

Second, *we must be watchful to prevent hard heartedness.* The writer of Hebrews warns, *"Take care,
brothers, lest there be in any of you an evil, unbelieving heart, leading you to fall away from the living God"*

(Heb. 3:12). Proverbs 28:14 reminds us, *"Blessed is the one who fears the LORD always, but whoever hardens his heart will fall into calamity"* (Prov. 28:14). Bold reformers carefully guard their interior lives to intentionally avoid anything that resembles hard heartedness.

Third, *we must be watchful to avoid the world, the flesh, and the devil.* The apostle John admonishes believers, *"Do not love the world or the things in the world. If anyone loves the world, the love of the Father is not in him. For all that is in the world—the desires of the flesh and the desires of the eyes and pride in possessions is not from the Father but is from the world"* (1 John 2:1-16).

Stand Firm in the Faith

God's Word is our field manual. It clearly sets forth the marching orders for bold reformers. 1 Corinthians 16:13 instructs us to stand firm in the faith. The Greek term, translated *stand firm*, means "to persevere, remain, or abide." The flavor here is to "hold the fort" and stand our ground. The Scripture is filled with admonitions to stand firm, as we saw in the last chapter.

Paul stresses the importance of *standing firm* in Philippians 4:1. He writes, *"Therefore, my brothers, whom I love and long for, my joy and crown, stand firm thus in the Lord, my beloved."* Paul uses the same Greek word, again translated as *stand firm*, as he did in 1 Corinthians 16:13. Both are written in the present tense, which indicates ongoing action. And both terms are in the imperative mood. In other words, our call is to consistently stand firm in the gospel.

Dennis Rainey reminds us that soldiers remain at their post, even in a hurricane. Rainey writes, "That's what a soldier does. He 'stands firm.' As a friend told me, 'If these men can stand guard over the dead, how much more important is it that I stand guard over the living—my wife and my children?'"[125] How much more, then, shall we guard the good deposit (1 Tim. 1:13-14), which has been entrusted to us as leaders in the church—which is the pillar and buttress of truth (1 Tim. 3:15).

Observe several motives for standing firm:

1. *A Biblical Reason*

The biblical motive for *standing firm* is this: The Bible demands it! 2 Thessalonians 2:15 says, "*So, then, brothers, stand firm and hold to the traditions that you were taught by us, either by our spoken word or by our letter.*" 1 Peter 5:12 admonishes believers to stand firm. Philippians 1:27-28a says, "*Only let your manner of life be worthy of the gospel of Christ so that whether I come and see you or am absent, I may hear of you that you are standing firm in one spirit, with one mind striving side by side for the faith of the gospel, and not frightened in anything by your opponents.*" Paul instructs the believers in Galatia to stand firm: "*For freedom*

---

125. Dennis Rainey, *Stepping Up: A Call to Courageous Manhood* (Little Rock: FamilyLife Publishing, 2011), Kindle edition, Loc. 553.

Christ has set us free; stand firm therefore, and do not submit again to a yoke of slavery" (Gal. 5:1). And Paul instructs the Ephesian believers to be strong in the Lord and *stand firm*: *"Therefore take up the whole armor of God, that you may be able to withstand in the evil day, and having done all, to stand firm"* (Eph. 6:13).

2. *A Practical Reason*

If we don't stand firm, we will get knocked down. The Bible describes the fate of a person who neglects this imperative. Ephesians 4:14 tells us that he will remain as a child and will be battered by *"every wind of doctrine."* If we don't stand firm, we will get knocked off our feet every time. Second Peter 3:17 warns, *"You therefore, beloved, knowing this beforehand, take care that you are not carried away with the error of lawless people and lose your own stability."*

We cannot overemphasize the importance of standing firm in the gospel. And standing firm in the gospel implies steadfast allegiance to doctrine. First Timothy 4:16 reminds us, *"Keep a close watch on yourself and on the teaching. Persist in this, for by so doing you will save both yourself and your hearers."* Paul's emphasis here is on doctrine. We must carefully guard the doctrinal sideboards in our gospel communities. Sound doctrine is essential for at least nine reasons:

- It is profitable (2 Tim. 3:16; Ps. 19:11).

- We are commanded to teach what accords with sound doctrine (1 Tim. 4:13; Titus 2:1).

- It is the means of encouragement and hope (Rom 15:4).

- It enables us to be good servants of Christ (1 Tim. 4:6).

- It protects us against false doctrine and worldly philosophy (Eph. 4:14; 2 Tim. 4:3).

- It guards us from apostasy (1 Tim. 4:1).

- It helps us refute those who oppose sound doctrine (Tit. 1:9).

- There is no salvation apart from sound doctrine (1 Tim. 4:16).

Historic Christianity is not a content-less faith. Rather, the Christian faith sets forth truth in propositions. "There can be no vital spirituality, without a sound theology," writes Donald Bloesch.[126] Yet, many Christians appear to be more interested in tolerance and political correctness than rightly dividing the word of truth. Some Christians seem completely uninterested in doctrinal matters altogether. Johnson warns, "A healthy Christianity cannot survive without theology, and theology must matter today, especially in our mindless and irrational culture."[127] Some have been hijacked by

---

126. Donald Bloesch, *Crumbling Foundations: Death and Rebirth in an Age of Upheaval* (Grand Rapids: Academic Books, 1984), 111. Cited in John H. Armstrong, *The Coming Evangelical Crisis* (Chicago: Moody Press, 1996), 57.
127. Gary L. W. Johnson, cited in ibid.

humanism; others have been deceived by selfishness. At the end of the day, some have capitulated; they have given up; they have surrendered. The white flag flutters shamefully in the postmodern *zeitgeist.*

The white flag of compromise made its steady ascent up the flagpole of liberalism as weak-kneed people began to compromise on the authority, inerrancy, inspiration, and infallibility of Scripture. Doctrinal deviators began to compromise the character of God by minimizing his sovereignty or marginalizing his justice or wrath. These cowardly men compromised the fundamental doctrines of the faith. In an effort to become relevant, they lost their theological nerve. The church continues to pay a high price for its cowardice.

3. *A Theological Reason*

Paul emphatically states our goal: namely, maturity. He reaffirms this goal in Colossians 1:28—"*Him we proclaim, warning everyone and teaching everyone with all wisdom, that we may present everyone mature in Christ.*" To aim for anything less is tantamount to theological compromise.

STRATEGIES FOR STANDING FIRM

At least three concrete strategies will encourage us as we commit ourselves to standing firm in the faith.

1. Remain Grounded in the Christian Faith

One way to stay grounded is to take every opportunity possible to grow in grace. Enroll in a theology class or a discipleship group at your local church. Spend extended time in the Word of God. Memorize the Word of God. Meditate on the Word of God. Listen to gospel-centered sermons. Read good Christian books that exalt the glory of God and focus on the cross work of the Lord Jesus Christ. Flee from man-centered, humanistic nonsense that flood most bookstores, even Christian bookstores.

2. Drive a Stake in the Ground

Make a commitment to persevering in the Christian faith. Jude 20-21 admonishes us, *"But you, beloved, building yourselves up in your most holy faith and praying in the Holy Spirit, keep yourselves in the love of God, waiting for the mercy of our Lord Jesus Christ that leads to eternal life."* Putting a stake in the ground is an act of the will. It involves an inner resolve which is fueled by the Holy Spirit and energized by the Word of God.

3. Lock Arms with Other People of God

Proverbs 27:17 says, *"Iron sharpens iron, and one man sharpens another."* Bold reformers do well to stand together in gospel communities with other godly folks who desire mutual accountability.

Polycarp is an example of a person who was grounded in the Christian faith. He drove his stake in the ground and knew the benefit of locking arms with like-minded people of God. The bishop of Smyrna was a godly man who was committed to standing firm in the faith. At the end of the day, his commitment to the gospel cost him his life.

As Justo L. Gonzalez relates, prior to Polycarp's martyrdom, the judge ordered him to cry, "'Out with the atheists!' Polycarp responded by pointing to the crowd and saying, 'Yes. Out with the atheists!' Again the judge promised that if he would swear by the emperor and curse Christ, he would be free to go. But Polycarp replied with words which would echo through the halls of church history and inspire generations of bold reformers: 'For eighty-six years I have served him, and he has done me no evil. How could I curse my king, who saved me?'"[128]

When the judge threatened to burn him alive, Polycarp simply answered that the fire about to be lit would only last a moment, whereas the eternal fire would never go out. After he was tied to the post in the pyre, he looked up and prayed aloud, "Lord Sovereign God...I thank you that you have deemed me worthy of this moment, so that, jointly with your martyrs, I may have a share in the cup of Christ...For this...I bless and glorify you."[129]

Polycarp understood the supreme priority of standing firm in the faith. He was unwavering in his final moments. He remained watchful. He bore

128. Cited in Justo L. Gonzalez, *The Story of Christianity, Vol. 1* (San Francisco: Harper Collins Publishers, 1984), 44.
129. Ibid., 44.

the marks of a bold reformer. Oh, that we as people of God might set the "spiritual thermometers" in our homes and in our churches. May God raise up a new generation of leaders like Polycarp and Luther—people of courage and boldness, men with a theological backbone and unshakeable integrity. May God raise up a new generation of people and Christian leaders who say what they mean and mean what they say, men and women who are unashamed of the gospel, believers who are utterly unwilling to compromise the truth, disciples who will forego the comforts of this life and burn at the stake for the sake of truth. Oh, that we would be Christians who make this kind of bold commitment: *We stand firm in the faith!*

Act Like Men

Paul continues to unpack the qualifications of a bold reformer and speaks directly to men with these instructions: *"Be watchful, stand firm in the faith, act like men, be strong"* (1 Cor. 16:13). He instructs us to *act like men*, an imperative verb that means "to behave with the wisdom and courage of a man—as opposed to a child." Paul is calling us to be manly men, to exhibit courage in the face of danger, to be brave in the midst of adversity.

A way to obey this imperative is to flee from passivity. Men are increasingly passive and cowardly. Men are failing to pick up the mantle of leadership that God has entrusted us with—both in the home and the church. Dennis Rainey alerts us to the curse of passivity: "Male passivity is a disease that robs a man of his purpose while it destroys marriages, ruins families, and spoils legacies. A passive man doesn't engage, he retreats. He neglects personal responsibility. At its core, passivity is cowardice."[130] The bold reformer recognizes passivity and runs in the opposite direction.

Genesis 2:15 provides the framework for men who seek to carry out this critical imperative: *"The LORD God took the man and put him in the garden of Eden to work it and keep it."* Richard Phillips refers to this as the "Masculine Mandate: to be spiritual men placed in real-world, God-defined relationships, as lords and servants under God, to bear God's fruit by serving and leading."[131] Bold reformers embrace this mandate to be real men, committed to concrete tasks for the glory of God.

We *act like men* by working, a term which means "to serve, labor, and cultivate."[132] We are called to work in the "field" that God has placed us in, according to his sovereign pleasure. "Christian men," writes Phillips, "should desire to cultivate something worthwhile for the glory of God and the well-being of their fellow men."[133] Christian men should cultivate human hearts. We should be in a position to influence, mentor, and disciple

---

130. Rainey, *Stepping Up: A Call to Courageous Manhood*, Loc. 500.
131. Richard Phillips, *The Masculine Mandate* (Lake Mary: Reformation Trust, 2010), 9.
132. Thanks to Richard Phillips for his covenantal insight.
133. Phillips, *The Masculine Mandate*, 13.

our children and people under our care (Eph. 6:4). Christian men are called to serve their wives (Eph. 5:25-30).

Additionally, we *act like men* by *keeping*. The Hebrew word translated as *keeping* means to "guard and protect." So Christian men are called to protect their families and nurture anyone in their care. Simply put, Christian men are called to lead to the glory of God. We must put the needs of others before our own. We must lead with integrity. We must lead with boldness. We must act like men.

The apostle Paul was the quintessential man. He was committed to the covenantal model of *working* and *keeping*. One of the prime ways Paul acted like a man was by maintaining an eternal perspective (2 Cor. 4:16-18). Paul was both tough and tender and he was a man with a God-centered perspective. As such, he was a bold reformer.

Be Strong

The final imperative in 1 Corinthians 16:13 is *be strong*. The term means "to strengthen or establish." The same word appears in Luke 2:40 and Ephesians 3:16. The term translated *strong* in this passage, like each of the other verbs, is written in the present tense, which suggests ongoing action. We are called to be strong on a consistent basis as we lead in the home, the church, and in the market-place of ideas. Spurgeon challenges men to be men of strength and conviction: "The time has come for sterner men than the willows of the stream can afford; we shall soon have to handle truth, not with kid gloves, but with gauntlets—the gauntlets of holy courage and integrity. Go on ye warriors of the cross, for the King is at the head of you...THE OLD FAITH MUST BE TRIUMPHANT."[134]

God has appointed men to lead in the home and in the church. When men act in a cowardly way, we disobey God, dishonor our wives, and do great damage to our children. How can we become men of increasing spiritual strength and fulfill the command before us? We must commit ourselves to three specific action steps:

1. *We must develop a theological backbone*
Bold reformers must develop strong biblical convictions that remain unmoved when the cultural winds begin to blow. Bold reformers know what they believe. They refuse to vacillate or compromise the truth. So we stand resolute, unwilling to buckle under the pressure. Our theological backbone can withstand any argument, any debate, and will persevere during the difficult days.

2. *We must develop an ethical backbone*
Additionally, bold reformers must be men of unwavering ethics. We are men of our word. Our word is our bond. When we look someone in the eye and shake their hand, we seal a given transaction with a word and a look. Honesty and integrity

---

134. Spurgeon, *Autobiography: Volume 1, The Early Years*, 480-481.

are the non-negotiable building blocks that make up the interior life of a bold reformer.

3. *We must be Micah 6:8 men*
The Word of God shows where true strength resides. Micah 6:8 says, *"He has told you, O man, what is good; and what does the LORD require of you but to do justice, and to love kindness, and to walk humbly with your God."* Bold reformers are at their best when they are walking in humility before God and before people. Samuel is an example of a man who stood strong despite opposing forces. He strengthened the Israelites as they faced their enemies (1 Sam. 4:9). He stood face-to-face against Saul when he sinned against the Lord (1 Sam. 15:17-23) and he dealt decisively with Agag (1 Sam. 15:32-33).

SUMMARIZING THE CALL

The call in 1 Corinthians 16:13 is a call to stand firm in the gospel. Paul emphasizes this mandate in 1 Corinthians 15:58. He writes, *"Therefore, my beloved brothers, be steadfast, immovable, always abounding in the work of the Lord, knowing that in the Lord your labor is not in vain."* Notice the three additional marks of a person who stands firm in the gospel:

Be Steadfast
The bold reformer is a steadfast person. The Greek term, translated *steadfast* (ESV) and *stand firm* (NIV), means to "be firm; not subject to change

or variation." The word has implications for our behavior. It involves standing firm on a given matter with conviction. It means to be settled on a matter.

In the broad context, Paul calls us to be steadfast in light of the resurrection of the Lord Jesus Christ. It is the resurrection that emboldens us and enables us to be steadfast and firm in a world system which rejects the gospel. The steadfast man is resolute, filled with bold resolve. He has a steady purpose, maintains steady goals, and builds firm convictions that are rooted in biblical reality.

Additionally, God calls us to stand firm in the message which has been taught and to hold fast to the word which has been preached: *"Now I would remind you, brothers, of the gospel I preached to you, which you received, in which you stand, and by which you are being saved, if you hold fast to the word I preached to you—unless you believed in vain"* (1 Cor. 15:1-2).

Immovable

Paul calls us to be immovable, a word that means "unshaken and steady." It describes a man who is "immovable, firm, and secure." Bold reformers remain rock-solid when the crowd capitulates. Bold reformers stand their ground when their friends and associates compromise. Nothing sways their single-minded affection for the Savior. Bold reformers are immovable.

Always Abounding in the Work of the Lord

This participle, *always abounding in the work of the Lord,* means "to have more than enough." It points to excessiveness. Paul has in mind a heart for ministry which is above and beyond, a ministry which is flourishing. Don't miss the object of this super-abounding verb, namely—"the work of the Lord." We should always be working for the Lord—diligently, passionately, and tirelessly. Unfortunately, a work ethic that is crippling Christians has crept into the church. But bold reformers know better. Our hearts are set on God's redemptive plan and our minds are anchored in God's Word. Our hands are grasping the plow and our feet are firmly planted in the field, which anticipates a great harvest in God's kingdom.

Paul emphasizes the call to stand firm in the gospel in Colossians 1:22. He writes, *"If indeed you continue in the faith, stable and steadfast, not shifting from the hope of the gospel that you heard, which has been proclaimed in all creation under heaven, and of which I, Paul, became a minister."*

The apostle sums up his argument in 1 Corinthians 15:58 by showing the anticipated result of the man who is steadfast, immoveable, and always abounding in the work of the Lord. He sounds this triumphant note: *"Your labor in the Lord is not in vain."* So, bold reformers, we must take heart! Our investment in God's Word and the lives of his people will not go unnoticed. Our labor matters. God is building his kingdom and he is using faithful people of God to accomplish his sovereign purposes!

*   *   *

Luther was a man committed to standing firm in the gospel. He stood fearlessly before the Roman Catholic Church when he nailed the ninety-five theses to the castle door at Wittenberg. He took his stand at the Diet of Worms and refused to compromise the truth. He stood on the solid rock of Scripture for the better part of a year in his time of seclusion at the Wartburg castle.

Luther was not a perfect man—far from it. Indeed, this man struggled with sins of omission and commission like any other person. Sometimes, his mouth got him in trouble. His quick wit and ability to "turn a phrase" led to moments of awkwardness and have proven to be a source of irritation for some people to this day. Some of his greatest strengths proved to be liabilities apart from the power of the Spirit. There are times when he appears to have "crossed the line" as he made his case for the cause of truth.

Yet, when truth was on the line, Martin Luther stood firm in the gospel. When the Bible was assaulted, Luther stood firm in the gospel. When he was personally attacked, he stood firm in the gospel. And when death was imminent, Luther stood firm in the gospel.

Oh, that the people of God would follow Luther's lead by standing firm in the gospel. May God raise up a new generation of leaders who will stand boldly in the marketplace of ideas and proclaim the truth. May he raise up a generation of people who boldly proclaim the truth from the pulpit. May the Holy Spirit rest on a band of believers who stand together for the cause of truth.

Epilogue

THE PATH OF THE BOLD REFORMER

Leadership is a lonely place. While leadership is typically very public, leaders often endure what seems like solitary confinement, a veritable torture chamber for the soul. Luther endured ten months of seclusion in the Wartburg castle. Thankfully, most leaders are not faced with such a drastic set of circumstances. However, the Wartburg experience is not totally foreign to leaders. Indeed, serving as a leader in the church of Jesus Christ is a lonely endeavor. It is a path that is at times paved by betrayal and backstabbing. Leaders bear a heavy weight and are sometimes burdened to the point of despair (2 Cor. 1:8). Leaders understand what Paul means when he speaks about the creation, which *groans* (Rom. 8:22). This world is not what God originally intended and leaders know this intuitively. They know it by experience and they have the battle scars to prove it.

Luther endured the loneliness of leadership, which was initiated by his bold move at Wittenberg in 1517, and persisted until his dying day in 1546. He was a hunted man and a hated man. He was mocked and maligned, taunted and tempted. Yet, Luther persevered during these difficult days. He outlasted his enemies and gained a few trusted friends along the way.

Martin Luther was not a perfect man. In fact, he was far from perfect. In a brilliant move, Carl Trueman identifies that Luther's strengths were also his weaknesses: "The hardheaded stubbornness and conviction that he was right—which meant he could face down the combined might of church and empire at Worms in 1521 and put the Wittenberg radicals to flight in 1522—was the same character trait that shaped his arrogant attacks on the Jews."[135] Luther's example, can in a very real way, inspire Christ-followers to be bold reformers, yet never in a way that denigrates people or destroys the reputation of the church. His example has the power to spur them on while at the same time remind them to keep Christ at the center of the affections.

Luther's ecclesiastical and academic achievements were nothing short of remarkable. His courageous leadership and gospel-centered convictions

---

135. Trueman, *Luther on the Christian Life*, 55.

helped fuel the Protestant Reformation and restore the Word of God to its rightful place. His efforts remain with us today as a growing number of evangelicals are discovering the treasure chest of Christ's gospel, the gospel that promises salvation to everyone who believes—by grace alone, through faith alone, in Christ alone, on the Word alone, to God be the glory alone!

Yet, we have learned a valuable lesson as we observe Luther's life: namely, ministry is not for the faint of heart. We may recognize the need for reform and sit alone in a boardroom or feel like an outsider in a crowded sanctuary. We may refuse to compromise the truth and pay dearly as church members walk away, one by one, shattering friendships and dreams of fruitfulness. We may refute the opposition with courage and boldness and be caricatured as "unloving" or "dogmatic." We may resist the world, the flesh, and the devil and rely on the power of the Holy Spirit, yet we continue in a life or death battle until we enter the gates of the Celestial City. We may remain focused on the plan of God and the promises of God but still meet stiff opposition along the way. We may rest in the sovereignty of God, which is to suggest that we stand in the minority as we fight for the cause of truth. We may rejoice in the hope of the gospel even when we cannot remember the last profession of faith. We may rejoice in the hope of the gospel even when the last baptism has faded from our memory. We may resolve to proclaim the gospel, yet find that many people are unwilling to listen, let alone believe. And we may remember to stand firm in the gospel even though most people are content to stand compliantly with the crowd.

In short, we may bear the marks of a bold reformer, yet wonder if we have what it takes to continue on and "carry the torch." Some days, the label *bold reformer* may appear as words on a page instead of a commitment of the heart. Other days may be filled with discouragement and heartache. The path of the bold reformer is lonely and labor-intensive. Yet it is a path worth tracing out as we strive to please our Commanding Officer.

In the months that followed the troubling days of the church I pastor, our troubles only intensified as people continued to leave the church. Some left out of a sense of frustration; others left because of doctrinal struggle, especially as it related to Reformed theology.

The path of the bold reformer will often be met with stiff opposition and trials, yet our great God is in providential control of all things. *Bold reformers must face every challenge in light of this glorious and God-centered reality. "Our God is in the heavens. He does all that he pleases"* (Ps. 115:3). His sovereign control over all things is not only a theological reality, but it is a veritable boon for the soul!

The path of the bold reformer is often filled with pain and suffering. Since bold reformers are leaders by definition, it should come as no surprise when adversaries shoot their arrows in our direction. Bold reformers commit their way to God and trust in his sovereign hand. The psalmist remarks, *"But I trust in you, O LORD; I say, 'You are my God.' My times are in your hand"* (Ps. 31:14-15a).

The path of the bold reformer may be marked with accusation, slander, and libel. Much like Nehemiah, reformers may be hindered by an opposing mob. Nehemiah chose to fear God and persevere in the work given to him by God (Neh. 5:15). The work of Nehemiah was blessed by God. Such is the lot of the bold reformer.

Now is the time for bold reformers to march decisively into the marketplace of ideas, bringing forth a message of hope and grace found in the gospel of Jesus Christ! These bold reformers must be willing to withstand opposition as God enables them by his sovereign grace. They must stand firm and exalt the great truths of the Reformed faith for every eye to see. They must herald the doctrines of grace so that every ear may hear.

Five hundred years ago, Martin Luther nailed his now famous ninety-five theses to the castle door in Wittenberg. Luther's courage continues to inspire faithful followers of Jesus. His character raises the bar for anyone who strives to serve with truth-centered passion in the kingdom of God. His conviction puts steely audacity in the hearts of the timid and fearlessness in the one prone to cowardice. The resolve of Martin Luther helps fuel a new generation of Christians who do the right things for the right reasons—all for the glory of God.

October 31, 2017 will mark the 500th year anniversary of the Protestant Reformation. This quincentennial celebration should be a time of great rejoicing. It should be a time to remember the accomplishments of Luther and the reformers. It should rouse us from our inactivity and awaken us to the beauty of the gospel. It should revive our affection for the Savior and it should refresh our love for the doctrines of grace. It should refuel our resolve to stand obediently before our sovereign God. Now is the time to celebrate the gospel-centered convictions of Martin Luther. To that end, the gospel will be triumphant as people of God treasure the truth of God in their hearts and minds. It is time for a new generation of bold reformers!

Soli Deo gloria!